Going round i

implementing and learning
from Circle Time

University
of Southampton | Hartle

Monica J. Taylor

Published in December 2003
by the National Foundation for Educational Research,
The Mere, Upton Park, Slough, Berks SL1 2DQ

ISBN 1 903880 57 2

Contents

Acknowledgements

This study would not have been possible without the initial cooperation of headteachers and key Circle Time teachers who took part in telephone interviews. Particular thanks are due to the headteachers, teachers and pupils in the 14 case study schools who allowed us to observe their Circle Time practices and talked about their experiences of implementing and what they learnt from Circle Time. In many of these schools Circle Time was a valued teaching and learning strategy in their provision for personal and social education.

I am grateful for assistance with two school visits from colleagues, Fiona Johnson and Anne Lines. At the outset of the project Clare Hill undertook some telephone interviews and accompanied me on a few school visits. Subsequently, for the duration of the project, Maxine Bailey carried out telephone calls with schools and proponents of Circle Time and undertook some data analysis.

In conclusion, I should like to thank Dr Joanna Le Métais for reading and making useful suggestions about the report and Jill Ware for secretarial support.

Author's note

Direct quotations are shown in italic and are indented. Examples that are not direct quotations are shown as indented roman text.

1 Circle Time as a strategy in personal and social education: origins, aims and claims

1.1 Introduction

In recent years Circle Time has become an increasingly popular teaching strategy, especially in primary schools. As part of a whole-school approach, it can demonstrate the school's provision for the spiritual, moral, social and cultural development of its pupils, by developing a caring ethos, teaching by example, encouraging democratic values and pro-social behaviour and including pupils in the formation of classroom rules. More specifically, it can be used in the primary classroom to enhance pupils' personal and social development and to introduce the key skills necessary for citizenship and language development.

Circle Time has several proponents, each with his/her own version of the technique and it has also been popular in North America and Europe. However, in the UK there has been very little published research on Circle Time and no independent evaluation of its effectiveness. Given the current political and professional interest in successful strategies of personal and social development and citizenship education, teachers and policy makers need to be better informed about the aims, use and effectiveness of Circle Time. Funded by NFER, this research aimed to explore provision and practice in Circle Time, consider teachers' aims in using it and describe the learning outcomes perceived by teachers and pupils in primary schools.

This opening chapter considers the nature and scope of Circle Time and examines its potential contribution to personal and social education and citizenship in primary schools. It offers an up-to-date summary of relevant research as a context for this project. Finally, the chapter describes the research project and outlines the structure of this report.

1.2 Circle Time: definition, origins and aims

1.2.1 What is Circle Time?

Circle Time is a strategy mostly used in primary schools, but it may equally be used with pre-school children (Rubinstein Reich, 1994), secondary students (Mosley, 1988, 1998b; Tew, 1998) or adults (Newton, 1995). Circle Time should be a carefully structured rule-bounded activity. Mosley (1993b, 1996), for example, emphasises the importance of structure, (comprising a warm up game, a round, an open forum, a celebration and closure). Each Circle Time group needs a few basic rules, which might be displayed in the class. Curry and Bromfield (1998:43) suggest:

- only one person talks at a time

- everyone else listens and shows this by looking at the person who is speaking

- everyone is included and has a turn

- everyone has a right to have fun

- no one can spoil anyone else's fun.

Typically, everyone, including the teacher, sits in a circle at the same level and shares ideas and feelings. An object, a shell or soft toy, for example, is passed around the circle, so that each individual has an opportunity to contribute. Only the person holding the object can speak. Participants can choose not to speak by saying 'pass'. Thinking time may be allowed, so at the end of the round pupils who have passed may be asked if they would now like to speak. Each speaker has the right to express personal views and opinions and to be listened to by others in the circle. Negative comments about other members of the group are not permitted.

The teacher may offer a starter phrase (e.g. 'When I come into class after break I feel ... '; or 'My favourite food is ... ') and may move on to a more serious discussion by inviting the children to suggest ways of resolving specific problems which have arisen in the class. This basic format may be varied in a number of ways, for example: by including teaching assistants, special needs assistants or parents in the circle; by dividing a whole class into smaller circles; by encouraging discussion in pairs or by broadening the range of activities to include games, singing and story telling.

Handbooks and manuals offer suggestions for organising and conducting Circle Time, for example, White (1991, 1998a and b), Mosley (1993b, 1996), Bliss and Tetley (1993), Bliss, Robinson and Maines (1995) and Curry and Bromfield (1994, 1998). Mosley (1992, 1993a; Lang and Mosley, 1993), in particular, has stressed its role as part of a whole-school approach to positive behaviour. Wald, Morris and Abraham (1996) indicate ways of involving very young children with diverse abilities. Goldthorpe and Mosley (1998) offer practical solutions to writing Individual Education Plans for pupils with emotional and behavioural problems and Mosley (1998a) provides photocopiable support materials.

Peter Lang (1998) provides a succinct account of some theoretical strands underpinning Circle Time, as practised internationally and in England. Jenny Mosley (1996:70–5) gives an account of the psychological and pedagogical influences on her approach. Lang outlines the origins of Circle Time as follows:

- The Magic Circle, originated in California in the 1960s–70s and focuses on the development of self-esteem of younger pupils in small groups

- Timmerman and Ballard (1975) describes it as an approach to humanistic education, underpinned by ideas from Rogers (1983) and Maslow (1968)

- Ballard (1982) describes it as a method in itself

- Dreikurs (1968) and Glasser (1969) stress the importance of classroom discussion concerning the conduct of the class and to change children's feelings or behaviour

- in Northern Europe, especially Sweden, Froebel influenced the development of Circle Time which, after World War Two, became a means of fostering democratic values as part of personal and social education

- in the Netherlands, a progressive school movement, 'Jenaplan', includes teaching and learning in a circle to facilitate democratic communication

- in Italy, Circle Time techniques are used in small groups with a training programme and evaluation to address disaffection.

Lang (1998:7) acknowledges the 'wide range of practice' described as Circle Time in England. First, Circle Time may be approached through writers/consultants (notably Mosley, White and Bliss, Robinson and Maines) who acknowledge influences from humanistic psychology, but are not specific about the theoretical underpinnings of their approaches. Second, there are those who promote Circle Time in practice, through activities. (Chapter 2, p. 15 outlines some more theoretical influences on writers/trainers.) Third, Circle Time has grown informally from school to school without their understanding the theoretical background or undertaking training. Lang perceives 'the increasing tendency to characterise Circle Time as a kind of therapy' (p. 9) and refers to the confusion in England between pedagogic and psychological approaches, which are differentiated elsewhere.

In the literature, approaches to Circle Time appear to share key characteristics and goals including: raising self-esteem, creating positive behaviour and cooperative classroom learning. Some accounts emphasise other aspects, such as social activities, acknowledging children's rights and feelings and encouraging pupil participation and using Circle Time to generate ideas for and discuss feedback from school councils. Further links are made with aspects of special needs education, such as 'circles of friends' (Whitaker *et al.*, 1998), to support the inclusion of students with disabilities such as autism, in mainstream classes. Others (Cowie and Sharp, 1992; DfE, 1994) report on the use of 'quality circles' – a technique used in industry to increase workforce participation – to involve pupils in seeking solutions to bullying.

Our inquiries revealed a range of other examples, such as:

- the Woodcraft Folk movement (1995), based on cooperation and global awareness, opens and closes its meetings with activities in a circle. Camping, games and discussion are carried out in a circle, which is used as a symbol of democracy and equality and to enhance group work, participation and decision-making skills

- the Kidscape Campaign for Children's Safety trains teachers to use Circle Time to address bullying

- the Anti-Bullying Network (2002) website has a section on Circle Time

- the Teachers Advisory Council for Alcohol and Drug Education (TACADE) training manual (Evans, 1990) outlines whole-school in-service training activities and suggests 'Ground Rules' for pupils similar to those used in Circle Time, as well as the skills needed by teachers (e.g. no 'put downs', don't 'pull rank', value all pupils' contributions, use confidentiality in discussion, listen rather than lecture)

- an evaluation of the Citizenship Foundation's materials *You, Me, Us!* (Taylor, Hill and Lines, 1998) found that many primary schools which used these materials, especially the topics on 'Friendship and Rules', also regularly used Circle Time.

1.2.2 Aims of Circle Time

Aims of Circle Time identified in the literature include:

- to develop self-knowledge and enhance confidence and self-esteem

- to develop the ability to share and discuss thoughts and feelings

- to develop empathy, cooperation, caring behaviour, respect for the feelings of others and a sense of belonging to a group or community

- to promote problem-solving and conflict resolution

- to develop trust, responsibility and other qualities of character

- to create shared rules endorsed by pupils, including sanctions and rewards which promote positive behaviour

- to develop skills of speaking and active listening, taking turns, questioning, hypothesising and critical reflection

- to encourage pupils to recognise their own worth and value and those of their peers

- to help pupils engage in personal reflection and clarify their own values.

If, as the literature suggests, the development of self-esteem is one of the main purposes of Circle Time, clarity about the concept of self-esteem is vital. Canfield (1990) and Damon (1991) link self-esteem with an increase in adjustment and happiness and also with the development of social responsibility. McMillan, Singh and Simonetta (1994) argue that positive self-esteem is most likely to develop when students learn concern and respect for others and 'obtain positive feedback following meaningful involvement and effort' (p.145).

1.3 Circle Time in relation to personal and social education and citizenship

This section considers the context of government policy on Personal and Social Education (PSE) and Citizenship relevant to Circle Time, evidence of increased use of Circle Time in primary school practice and inspection comments about the contribution of Circle Time to PSE in primary education.

1.3.1 Personal and social education and citizenship in the primary school

PSE has always been a central feature of the work of primary schools. In the past, this was often loosely characterised by the description 'caring and sharing'. Ofsted inspections and National Curriculum reforms require primary schools to clarify their provision for pupils' personal and social development. The Government appointed advisory groups on citizenship and the teaching of democracy in schools (Crick, 1998) and on personal, social and health education (PSHE) (DfEE. NAGPSHE, 1999).

The Citizenship Advisory Group's final report (Crick, 1998) sets out a clear definition of citizenship education and recommends a statutory a framework for its delivery. The definition of 'effective education for citizenship' focuses on three separate but interrelated strands.

1. Social and moral responsibility: children learn from the very beginning self-confidence and socially and morally responsible behaviour both in and beyond the classroom, both towards those in authority and towards each other.

2. Community involvement: pupils learning about and becoming helpfully involved in the life and concerns of their communities, including learning through community involvement and service to the community.

3. Political literacy: pupils learning about how to make themselves effective in public life through knowledge, skills and values. (Crick, 1998:40–1).

The Advisory Committee advocated that these three strands should be developed progressively through a young person's education and training experiences, from pre-school to adulthood. Clearly, the primary phase is

6

likely to focus on the development of social and moral responsibility and some aspects of community involvement and, by means of their involvement in their school community, primary pupils' nascent political literacy. Some suggested learning outcomes can be partly met through Circle Time, for example, at key stage 1:

- express and justify orally a personal opinion ...

- contribute to ... discussion, ... learning what it means to take turns, respond to the views of others and use acceptable forms of disagreement or challenge

- use imagination when considering the experience of others

- know about the nature and basis of the rules in the classroom ... and know how to frame rules themselves ...

- understand the language used to describe feelings associated with aspects of relationships with others ...

- understand different kinds of behaviour using moral categories such as kind or unkind, good or bad, right or wrong; know about the consequences of anti-social or egocentric behaviour and attitudes, for individuals and communities; also understand that many problems can be tackled as a community

- know about differences and similarities between people in terms of their needs, rights, responsibilities, wants, likes, values and beliefs; know and understand through shared activities and the process of exploratory talk, the meaning of key terms such as respect or disrespect ... (Crick, 1998:46–7).

The recommendations of the Crick Report have prevailed over those of other advisory committees. Since August 2000, citizenship has been part of a non-statutory framework for personal, social and health education (PSHE) at key stage 1 (age five to seven) and key stage 2 (age seven to 11). The framework has four components, including an outline of the knowledge, skills and understanding to be taught. Two aspects, 'developing confidence and responsibility and making the most of their abilities' and 'developing good relationships and respecting the differences between people' could be seen as central to Circle Time. The framework includes links with the National Healthy School Standard, recommends a whole-school approach and suggests how PSHE and Citizenship can be taken forward flexibly to suit the school's own context

(QCA, 2000). It refers to Circle Time as a means of helping children develop a behaviour policy (p.10). Guidance for Citizenship at key stage 1 and 2, Unit 1 'Taking part – developing skills of communication and participation' may be seen as especially relevant to Circle Time (QCA, 2002). Proponents of Circle Time have also pointed out that it addresses components in English Attainment Target One in speaking and listening, especially turn taking, waiting for a response and listening attentively (e.g. see Curry and Bromfield, 1994:8).

1.3.2 Primary practice

In recent years Circle Time has become an increasingly popular strategy. A national survey of values education in 1997 found that Circle Time was included in staff development in 184 of the 337 primary schools responding (Taylor, 2000). In a national survey of the use of discretionary time in 161 primary schools (Galton and Fogelman, 1998:126) almost half of the headteachers reported that Circle Time was the most frequent PSE activity for year 1. By year 6 Circle Time was still fairly common as an activity in discretionary time, though only in about 15 per cent of schools. More primary schools reported using Circle Time than engaging in health or citizenship education activities.

Circle Time is also used in conjunction with other school-based activities and approaches to personal and social development. White (1998, 1990) reports on the introduction of Circle Time in primary schools and some effects on pupils. Campbell and Dominy (1997) describe how Circle Time functions as part of PSE to promote positive attitudes and to counter racism.

1.3.3 Circle Time and PSE: evidence from inspection

Ofsted reports frequently comment on primary schools' use of Circle Time, mainly under the heading 'Pupils' spiritual, moral, social and cultural development' or 'Children's attitudes, behaviour and personal development'. A report on the use of Circle Time in Wiltshire primary schools (Dawson and McNess, 1998:6) found that over four-fifths of schools responding (half of all schools) had had Ofsted reports and approximately one-third of these reports had made reference to Circle Time.

Several schools in this research mentioned positive comments from Ofsted in their school inspection reports (see also Appendix 2). Comments from Ofsted reports in four survey schools included:

Good use is made of circle time to raise self-esteem, promote positive attitudes towards others and helps to lay a good foundation for the development of citizenship.

Circle time is used in some classes for children to consider the views of others and to work together for the benefit of the school community.

Class discussions at circle time provide good opportunities for pupils to explain what makes them feel as they do about topics such as poverty or the destruction of the environment.

The spiritual awareness of the pupils is developed through experiences and opportunities for reflection during discussion in circle times and most assemblies, as well as through lessons in English, dance, religious education and music. The pupils respond well to these experiences. The highly effective use of circle time and other informal opportunities for discussion allows the pupils to address issues of right and wrong, and responsibility for themselves, others and the environment in a positive and non-judgmental atmosphere.

This NFER research shows that in a few schools the use of Circle Time had contributed to gaining an Investor in People Award. The 'most improved' primary school in 2001–2 included raising pupils' self-esteem, through Circle Time and other personal and social education strategies (e.g. Golden Time and a playground Buddy System), as well as improving teaching and monitoring pupils' progress, among its key improvement techniques (Hall, 2002).

1.4 Summary of research on Circle Time

A critical review of research for Ofsted (Halstead and Taylor, 2000) identified Circle Time as one of the key aspects of values education in need of further exploration. Many claims have been made for the potential of Circle Time to enhance learning but empirical evidence has been lacking. There is no known major published research nor independent evaluation in the UK of its effectiveness. However, a body of literature and small-scale research have recently emerged. The overview of research offered here is based on (and updates) Halstead and Taylor's work (Halstead and Taylor, 2000:Key Topic 15).

1.4.1 Qualitative research

A small-scale research project carried out by Hall in 1994 into the attitudes of nine- and ten-year-olds and their teachers towards Circle Time confirms its potential for developing problem-solving skills and enhancing self-concept and self-esteem (reported in Lang, 1996).

A study of the social and educational content of Circle Time based on interviews with Swedish teachers and children suggested that Circle Time was generally thought to contribute to the development of personal identity, to increase self-awareness, to foster democratic values and to train children in the complicated rules of social interaction. However, whereas teachers saw Circle Time as directed towards caring and a feeling of togetherness, young children talked more of the self-restraint and having to sit still (Reich, 1994).

Lown (2002) reports on a small-scale study in one LEA where Circle Time was introduced as part of an accredited training course addressing behavioural and emotional needs to reduce exclusions. Teachers and pupils (mainly primary) largely agreed that there had been improvements in listening, cooperative and turn taking skills, self-esteem and ability to express feelings. Children appreciated the opportunity to work with others beyond their friendship group and teachers felt they had a better understanding of the children. Circle Time also appeared to have some beneficial effects on wider groupwork activities.

1.4.2 Experimental research

Despite the increasingly popular use of Circle Time, there is little research which seeks to evaluate its effectiveness. In 1979–80, specific materials for use in Circle Time were tested with first-graders in Missouri and were found to have a significant effect on the development of their self-concept and motivation (Dixon, 1981). Mosley (1988) reported positive responses from a group of lower secondary students to a five-week Circle Time intervention in a tutorial period. Tew (1998) reported on the use of Circle Time to teach PSE compared with a year 7 group receiving other forms of PSE with a highly experienced teacher. Students perceived the Circle Time to be worthwhile and a relevant method for teaching PSE. They had benefited individually and as a group and were more aware of the learning process.

Curry (1997) found that Circle Time provided emotional support which led to the reintegration of a ten year-old girl with emotional and behavioural disorders. Kelly (1999) reported on a whole-class and withdrawal-group intervention using Circle Time in a primary school with a significant number of pupils with emotional and behavioural difficulties. The majority of targeted children showed positive behavioural change, but the whole-class approach was most effective. Concerned about the poor quality of relationships within their year 6 class, two teachers (Moss and Wilson, 1998) conducted an intervention study using seven planned weekly Circle Time sessions focusing on relationships and feelings. Pre- and post-evaluative questionnaires and sociometric measures showed that at the end of the study pupils expressed more positive feelings and fewer negative feelings about others in the class. The authors suggested the value of a proactive rather than a reactive approach.

1.4.3 Related research

Research into other discussion-based methods of teaching indicates that:

- children feel more secure and less vulnerable if there are clear ground rules, including not interrupting, not making negative comments about others and avoiding racist and sexist statements. Rules are more effective if negotiated with pupils (Chamberlain, 1992)

- teachers may sometimes reduce questions without adversely affecting either child utterances or class behaviour. Replacing questions with praise may increase children's contributions (Moore, Knott and McNaughton, 1989) but the most effective praise is specific, spontaneous, sincere and discriminating (Brophy, 1981)

- the success of any discussion-based activity depends on participants' attitudes and interpersonal skills (Lucas and Jenkins, 1988) and teachers need to be aware that pupils often do not perceive talk and discussion to be valuable learning modes (Hall, 1995)

- the development of dialogue between teachers and students and between students is part of the education of the emotions; students see listening as central to relationships for learning and emotional development (McLaughlin, 2000).

1.4.4 Expert advice

Housego and Burns (1994) advise that Circle Time is most effective if its underlying values are in harmony with the general ethos of the classroom. They also point out that if the quality of Circle Time is to be maintained, pupils must be discouraged from offering superficial contributions and must be encouraged to think carefully and build on what has been said before. Dixon (1981) and Lang (1996) suggest that the attitude, enthusiasm and social and communicative competence of the teacher are vital to the success of Circle Time and Reich (1994) notes that this has clear implications for teacher training. Among the most significant findings of a survey of headteachers in Wiltshire primary schools (Tew, unpublished) was that half of them thought only 'particular teachers' were able to use Circle Time in the classroom, yet almost all saw Circle Time as having a positive effect on the ethos of the school and half thought it had a major impact on children's behaviour. Cremin (2002), an experienced consultant in developing Circle Time in primary and secondary schools, suggests that Circle Time is sometimes neglected and ineffective for a range of reasons: lack of time due to the standards agenda and Ofsted; societal attitudes towards power, control and children; lack of teacher training in leading Circle Time sessions; inadequate resources and the lack of a whole-school, developmental approach to PSHE and Circle Time.

1.5 The research project

This section presents the rationale, aims and methodology of the research.

1.5.1 Relevance

As noted earlier, published research is mostly descriptive and focuses on practical and operational issues. Promoters of Circle Time have sponsored some unpublished research (Mosley, 1998c; Tew, unpublished). Existing research has not offered an opportunity to hear the reflections of the teachers and pupils on their experiences and learning. It has also not previously explored, through triangulation of perspectives, the different meanings which may be given to perceptions of Circle Time.

1.5.2 Aims of the research

The NFER funded this project to investigate aims, uses and perceptions of effectiveness of Circle Time and to provide an independent review of a common strategy about which little is known other than in particular schools and classes. The general purposes of the research were to:

- raise awareness of ways in which Circle Time as a strategy is used by primary teachers in the UK

- provide examples of positive practice of Circle Time in use

- ascertain teachers' and pupils' perceptions of learning from Circle Time across a number of skill areas basic to personal, social and moral interaction.

More specifically, the project explores aims for and teaching and learning outcomes of Circle Time; evaluates the use of the strategy; offers positive examples of practice and reviews implications for whole-school development and training.

1.5.3 Research method and sources

The research utilised a qualitative case study methodology grounded in a quantitative telephone survey of a national sample of schools. The project was conducted over two terms, which facilitated a methodology of breadth and some depth. It draws upon four main sources of data:

1. a review of the research literature on Circle Time and the curriculum materials available to teachers

2. contact with the main authors and trainers in Circle Time in the UK to gain a sense of the development of the technique and its theoretical associations, their own emphases in training and concerns about school implementation and perceptions of outcomes

3. telephone interviews with 57 primary headteachers and key Circle Time teachers on their perceptions of its aims, use and effectiveness

4. case studies in 14 of these schools which appeared to use different models of Circle Time, for which they undertook training and planning and which teachers claimed contributed to PSE and learning outcomes for pupils.

For further information about the research methodology, sampling, school selection, telephone survey and case studies, see Appendix 1.

1.5.4 Structure of the report

Chapter 2 considers strategic perspectives on and interpretations of Circle Time, drawing on the telephone and face-to-face interview data from Circle Time proponents and trainers. Senior Managers in a national telephone survey of primary schools provide information on their rationale and perceptions of Circle Time in their schools.

Chapter 3 draws upon the case studies of class teachers' aims for Circle Time and its provision through several models of delivery.

Chapter 4 focuses on issues which arise in the delivery of Circle Time, which include organisational matters, the role of the teacher, the participation of pupils and ethical concerns of sensitivity, confidentiality and disclosure in the circle. We offer some critical reflections on some values and pedagogical issues.

Chapter 5 deals with class teachers' learning and perceptions from conducting Circle Time. We review their reflections on their experiences of training and compare this with their on-the-job learning by doing Circle Time. Teachers told us about their learning about their pupils and what they considered them to have learnt from Circle Time experiences. We also explored with teachers their perceptions of the implications of doing Circle Time for the school as a whole, including liaison with parents.

In Chapter 6 we address, through their voices, pupils' understanding, experiences and perceptions of Circle Time, including the group process, practical concerns, rules and personal boundaries. Children's perceptions of Circle Time and their likes and dislikes are explored. The pupils also describe their personal and social learning from Circle Time.

Chapter 7 offers some guidelines for Circle Time, to assist schools setting up or reviewing their Circle Time practices. In conclusion, Circle Time is evaluated as a strategy for personal and social education and citizenship and implications for pupil learning and pedagogical change are considered.

The References list the sources used and the Appendices provide details of the research methodology and the case study schools.

2　Strategic perspectives and interpretations

The literature on Circle Time identified organisations and individuals offering manuals and training in Circle Time and related circle group work. It was considered important to contact some of these proponents. In parallel a national telephone survey was conducted of senior managers and key Circle Time teachers in primary schools about their aims, training, provision for and views on Circle Time. This formed the framework for the more in-depth research in the case study schools (see Chapters 3 to 6).

2.1　Circle Time in principle: proponents' intentions, emphases, concerns and claims

Through contacts with ten key proponents of Circle Time (see Appendix 1), the research aimed to augment understanding gained from the review of the literature and handbooks and to increase awareness of their perceptions of the aims, use and effectiveness of training and of the issues arising in implementation. In particular, the research attempted to gain a sense of the history and evolution of the technique and how it has been interpreted and developed by key proponents and implemented in training.

The interviews covered a common core of questions on the theoretical basis of Circle Time, specific emphases in their approach, concerns and perceptions of the benefits and outcomes of using Circle Time in schools.

2.1.1　Theoretical basis of Circle Time

Some proponents of Circle Time, especially trainers, thought it was important to try to ascertain the psychological and theoretical underpinnings of Circle Time as this interviewee indicated:

> *It's a model in teaching. It is annoying when people ... come along and claim to have invented it. It derives from the US from the 70s – people like Ballard, Timmerman and Ballard, Carl Rogers. Now it is just being adapted by others. It is very misleading to say that they*

developed it. It is a bottom up thing happening without leadership.
Publications have tried to show how to 'do' Circle Time and undone a
lot of good work.

(Teacher trainer in a college of higher education)

The main theoretical influences in Circle Time identified by interviewees
were:

- person-centred approaches. Humanistic psychological approaches,
such as work by Timmerman and Ballard (1975), Ballard (1982) and
Rogers (1983) on the development of the capacity for growth and self-
understanding

- groupwork approaches were mentioned by several respondents. An
influential strand for one writer/trainer was the idea of social
interaction contributing to self-development through psychodrama and
sociodrama (e.g. Moreno, 1970) and developmental group work in
education undertaken by Leslie Button (1976) and Thacker, Stoate and
Feest (1992)

- democratic methods linked with William Glasser's (1969) work on
class meetings

- student-centred learning. Work by Brandes and Ginnis (1990) on the
student-centred school and Gallas on languages of childhood (1994,
1997) were cited as influential.

Other influential strands mentioned were: 'making it safe for children to
say things'; educational psychology for social responsibility, e.g. through
emotional literacy (Goleman, 1996); health and social services'
therapeutic approaches to promote equality and community 'we're in this
together'; social inclusion and assertive discipline and behaviour
management. Circle work undertaken by Quakers, Oxfam, Woodcraft and
UNICEF was mentioned in connection with conflict resolution.

It is not without interest that several of the proponents and trainers
interviewed, especially those who had written manuals, had similar
backgrounds in special needs education, particularly relating to
emotional and behavioural disorders, counselling, PSHE and sometimes
drama.

Related to the question of the theoretical background of 'Circle Time' is the issue of definition of 'Circle Time'. Proponents and trainers agreed that Circle Time could mean very different things in practice, though these might have a 'family resemblance'. 'Some teachers say they are doing Circle Time, but it depends on how you define Circle Time', remarked one interviewee.

> *There is no definition. If you do that then it won't get used. Intervention is problem-solving, not just using a book. It is quite personal and is difficult to do unless it's been part of your learning process. On our MA course we run courses on effective communication including group interaction which is part of Circle Time.*
>
> (Teacher trainer in higher education)

There was some recognition that one or two proponents of Circle Time had 'defined a clear model', though some saw this as behaviouristic. Others had placed more emphasis on activities than structure. A few proponents practised a more therapeutic approach, using the circle as 'transitional and transactional space' and through 'an open dialogue with practitioners' to lead to 'a certain vulnerability'.

Some considered the work in Circle Time as related to other work in circles.

> *Shape of the circle is crucial. A rounded square may not work for the children. They also need to be equidistant from the centre. Visually they need to be able to see everyone and make eye contact and to know that people can look at them. The circle is also important for listening.*
>
> (Writer/trainer)

Another writer/trainer saw the circle as 'a universal symbol' whose strengths included 'that it promotes eye contact, has cultural value and is necessary for genuine debate'.

2.1.2 Specific emphases of Circle Time in writers and trainers' approaches

The trainers' involvement with teachers and schools varied and included:

- private consultants working with the whole school, both the teaching and non-teaching staff, in school or occasionally in the organisation's headquarters, sometimes over a period of time. Some trainers worked in several schools at a time or with a cluster of schools, once or occasionally over a short period. A few trainers worked or preferred to work intensively with one school at a time, using a whole-school approach

- initial teacher training or MA courses, which included Circle Time

- in-service training in the LEA which focused on or included Circle Time as part of a PSHE or teaching methods course; this was then cascaded by participants to colleagues in school.

One PSHE trainer considered the role of the PSHE coordinator was vital to disseminating Circle Time:

> *I think that you need a [PSHE] coordinator in schools to make sure that good ideas are shared between teachers. I think at the moment this is a problem, I think to a lot of teachers the classroom is their kingdom.*
>
> (PSHE trainer)

- in-school INSET by a private consultant or LEA adviser or trainer.

Within school approaches to training included: working with a class group with their teacher as an observer; introducing the class teacher (and sometimes teaching assistants) to Circle Time through team-teaching; managing or orchestrating Circle Time through the teacher.

Another approach focused on problem-solving:

> *In anti-bullying we work with all the children, the whole school. We must enable the personal development of all children and avoid the word 'bullying'. As a group we want to increase their personal development and social skills, and this is done through Circle Time. The children feel safe in Circle Time, and like to discuss things which are concerning them. In terms of anti-bullying it is good as it is a group activity and brings it out in the open.*
>
> (Charity freelance trainer)

Some trainers worked across several schools at a time or with a cluster of schools, some times once or occasionally over a short period. A few trainers only worked, or preferred to work, intensively with one school at a time, in a whole-school approach.

Two trainers emphasised a whole-school approach:

> *We run training in establishing Circle Time and giving advice on managing it as a whole-school approach. It is not something to be undertaken lightly and should not encourage disclosure. It should be managed as a whole-school approach to promote behaviour. Its role is to establish a common understanding about behaviour and rules in the school. It can also be used to assess how these rules are going and reflect on things which are happening in the school, and also make suggestions for improvement ... We give schools access to a wide range of resources. We mainly point them to the direction of those which develop whole-school approaches, rather than those with just activities.*
>
> (LEA trainer)

A PSHE consultant and trainer for primary and secondary schools had developed an intensive approach:

> *I will go and work with kids and take Circle Time sessions with them to show the teachers it in action. I will only work with one school at a time and try to get the feel of the school. I also do follow-up sessions because I am concerned that after training there may be bad mistakes. I follow-up even up to 18 months later. I want to make sure that they understand the philosophy and underlying principles. The whole school needs to be looked at not just the class. An important part of my training is to get teachers to reflect. I also do counselling and so understand how Circle Time can be threatening for some. ... I spend a whole day, sometimes two, training. I look at the principles around Circle Time, how it helps self-esteem and listening, group dynamics, ground rules and then doing a practical session. I also try do to a session for parents and include all members of staff in my training from secretaries and dinner ladies to caretakers.*
>
> (PSHE consultant and trainer)

This trainer had also worked with playworkers and youth services using Circle Time and had introduced drama, role-plays, story telling, art work and puppets into Circle Time.

Two groupwork trainers sometimes used Circle Time with a teacher and her class as part of a broader psychotherapeutic approach, which focuses on talk and communication, 'legitimating the expression of feeling and the discovery of personal identity through social interaction'. In this case, the leadership role (symbolised by a badge or sash) is transferred from the teacher to one trainer, who leads the Circle Time, while the teacher is involved in the circle, observing and participating in the experience. The other trainer accompanies a child or children with whom she has worked and looks out for others who may have difficulties coping emotionally. Such Circle Times are part of an ongoing whole-school process. These trainers described themselves as 'interested in the moral and spiritual quality of a good circle' and 'more involved in narrative styles and processes' rather than 'a series of rituals, games and procedures', as 'the class is a community which has its own story to tell.' These trainers were interested in 'how genuine the encounter is and whether it can be continued or transferred.' The circle is 'an ethos in which collaboration is possible'.

By comparison, two interviewees, both writer/trainers, stressed the significance of structure in Circle Time. One suggested a model structure: a game, a round, an activity, a conference and an end game. She acknowledged that 'It is not everyone's comfort zone to do Circle Time', emphasised the importance of follow-up questioning and the need to model this to teachers. She recognised that teachers also needed guidance on how to deal with sensitive issues mentioned by children.

The second writer/trainer, acknowledged that 'Circle Time has power for destruction as well as power for the positive'. In her view, the game, round, open forum, celebration of success or offer of help and endgame all help with the ground rules. She claimed the method is adaptable and transferable to other curriculum areas and that skills are learned through the process. The school needs to focus on moral values, roles and sanctions, translating the issues talked about in Circle Time into practical action. She stressed the positive, e.g. instead of 'Don't run' say 'Walk in'.

One writer/trainer demonstrated Circle Time with 27 year 6 pupils at a national conference. The activity included a question: How do you feel when you have made a mistake?; a game 'All Have Numbers'; rules and an exercise 'I Don't Like it When … ' which involved helping a boy who had mentioned hitting a teacher by identifying behavioural goals for him and themselves. The pupils then told each other what they liked about the suggestions and what made them pleased in class.

She then debriefed the group, including the teacher, and answered questions from the large audience. During this charismatic and impressive performance the trainer emphasised several points:

- preparation of the group about what would be happening and debriefing about what did happen

- being inclusive of the whole group

- outlining the skills involved in the process: thinking, looking, speaking, listening and concentrating

- keeping anonymity :'In Circle Time we never say the name of anyone, I don't want anyone's feelings hurt'

- getting to know what people think so they can improve and be more cooperative; giving much positive reinforcement

- keeping up a pace

- involving a range of activities, including some physical coordination

- keeping a good mood in the group

- the teacher's self-esteem needs to be good

- negotiating the values promoted through Circle Time with all staff.

This trainer stressed the importance of five main structures and processes in Circle Time.

- Game. A physical activity, learning to work as a team and more harmoniously.

- A round. This is to demonstrate trust, learn turn taking and pupils developing confidence to speak and hear their own voices.

- Hold an open forum related to various mentioned or previously known issues. This can facilitate the creation of a culture of mutual support to empower children to address behavioural needs. Can relate to an action plan for class or individuals or peer recognition and achievement certificates.

- Celebrate success (otherwise the Circle Time would focus on problems).

- An Ending Ritual. Celebrate being together as a community. Enjoy a game and have fun.

Follow-up to training

One issue raised by the trainers was the need for teachers to follow up training, either through self-support methods in school (resources, evaluation, discussion with colleagues, further training) or with trainers (see also p. 19).

> *Circle Time is just one element of a wider brief. There is no time allocated to do follow up work as we are income-generating. The way we evaluate is through working with all our schools, looking at their Ofsted and general LEA monitoring.*
>
> (LEA trainer)

Whole-school involvement

Some trainers held the strong view that 'Circle Time is only effective if it is taken on by the whole school'. One trainer said a benefit of the whole-school approach is that 'it's circular'. Another trainer thought that it was very important that effective discipline and pastoral systems should be in place as the background context for Circle Time.

Thus one of the main issues identified by trainers was how to develop Circle Time as part of an integrated whole-school approach. Key points frequently mentioned were the need to link Circle Time with class and school rules, assemblies and school councils and to include parents and support staff, thus developing both a more collective and personal sense of responsibility. Most of the trainers, especially those who had not written manuals or handbooks, claimed to be eclectic about the resources they recommended to teachers. Some resources, listed in the References, were frequently mentioned.

2.1.3 Proponents' concerns about using Circle Time in schools

The trainers and writers identified several concerns about the way in which they perceived Circle Time to be implemented in schools.

The importance of training

Some teachers were implementing Circle Time without training:

> *It is a problem that teachers hear of a good thing, buy a book and just work from that. But there is more to Circle Time than a book. You need to see the right kind of facilitation and if not, you see bad Circle Times.*
>
> (Manual writer and trainer)

22

Misuse of Circle Time

One trainer said:

> *The negative aspect of Circle Time is that primary teachers may say they're using it, but they are misusing it. ... The fact that the children are sat on the carpet in front of them does not mean it is Circle Time. .... With teachers we might get in a circle and talk about how we use Circle Time. ... I might give examples of how to introduce it to children. ... I usually use some of Murray White's examples.*
>
> (Charity freelance trainer)

Another trainer stressed the need to stand aside and facilitate, rather than direct the Circle Time:

> *Bad practice is where a session is all teacher-directed because some are scared of losing that teacher role/position. When teachers sit on a different level to pupils it's appalling.*
>
> (Trainer)

A teaching method and/or a way of doing PSE?

Circle Time was seen by some teachers as a specific time or aspect of the curriculum, to replace PSHE. However, some proponents considered Circle Time as a distinct teaching method, and others emphasised it as an integral part of PSHE.

> *It shouldn't be seen as just special time but as a teaching method. It is not just part of PSE, but a teaching method. Once kids become used to it the more they take it over the better.*
>
> (An initial teacher trainer)

> *My concern about Circle Time is that it is seen in isolation. PSHE methodology consists of all different things which can be used and Circle Time is just one of them. If you just take Circle Time in its own right as a thing, you distract from it being part of this methodology.*
>
> (Freelance trainer)

One trainer felt that teachers should be able to sustain their method and develop it for themselves: 'If Circle Time just stays as "be nice to each other" then its use is very limited.' There was also concern about using Circle Time in an unstructured way with no content.

Teachers' personal and social characteristics

The teacher's psychological attitude, and willingness to give something of her/himself was deemed important in implementation: 'Circle Time needs personal investment from the teacher.' One trainer/author contrasted two types of teacher: the charismatic teacher, who could inspire and generate enthusiasm among others and the teacher whose own self-esteem needed improving before s/he could raise the children's self-esteem.

> *... one lady went back to her school and the whole school adopted it because she was so brilliant at Circle Time. She then went on to two other schools and developed it there also. If teachers see good practice they ask questions and are very interested. ... some teachers are apprehensive... because of their own [low] self-esteem and this is certainly a stumbling block. When I started advertising [as a trainer] I did so offering self-esteem for children, but actually it was really all about the teachers.*
>
> (Trainer/author)

Another PSHE trainer noted:

> *Teachers need to share things in Circle Time and I think that a lot of them find this hard to do. I've seen some teachers who can't even complete rounds themselves such as 'I feel happy when... '. The other problem is if teachers use Circle Time as a manipulative tool, for example saying 'I feel unhappy when I see bullying'.*
>
> (PSHE trainer)

The relationship between teacher and pupils, the degree of 'safety' felt by the children and their trust in the circle were also considered important.

The pupils' response

A PSHE trainer had some concerns about some of the pupils who might be disadvantaged in the circle:

> *I think that you need to be careful with the quieter ones, I worry if they are pushed. I think that prior warning should be given to such children and those who speak English as a second language. Also in the Circle they should have a friend or careworker, or puppet who they can talk through. It amazes me though when some of the quieter ones talk. It is also a worry when some of them are very talkative.*
>
> (PSHE trainer)

Amount of time

One trainer said:

> *I think that Circle Time should be used at most once a week, if you overdo it I think it loses its specialness. With the smaller children sessions are 20 mins, with the older 40 mins.*
>
> (Trainer)

'Passing'

Children's use of and need for passing varied. One writer/trainer noted that 'holding the object is a way of having some power'. She cited three girls who held on to an object for too long without speaking until they 'passed', but did speak when she returned to them at the end of the round. When she stopped returning to them, they spoke first time. She was apprehensive about introducing the idea of passing too early into the group as she thought it important to get to know the children. She had worked with twins in a Circle Time; one had spoken straightaway, whereas the other had spent one and a half terms passing the object before she had found a voice.

Confidentiality

Confidentiality and anonymity in the circle were stressed by some respondents as being important, intrinsically and for group bonding.

Therapy?

Opinions about the role of Circle Time as a therapeutic activity seemed to relate to the approach adopted by the trainer or training organisation. One publisher/trainer felt that 'teachers do need training in psychotherapy', but an LEA trainer said:

> [Circle Time] *is not a therapeutic activity and it certainly shouldn't be 'no holds barred'. It should not explore deeply psychological issues or individual casework. Pupils can raise issues, but they should be able to do so in a structured way and should know what will happen.*
>
> (LEA trainer)

2.1.4 Perceived benefits and outcomes

Most trainers were aware of some schools' reports that Circle Time had had a considerable effect. There seemed to be common agreement that it could contribute to improving behaviour and raising self-esteem. Some proponents and trainers also noted Circle Time's contribution to enhancing communication skills, developing caring and empathy, resolving difficulties and creating a sense of belonging.

Another author claimed:

Over time you see a change, who has developed a voice and who has not. Children get a sense of fairness and that everyone has a right to speak. Circle Time can empower the quiet and withdrawn children as they are given more respect and consideration. It can also benefit the children who act out more as they begin to learn the business of friendship, taking turns and joining in through the modelling of appropriate behaviour. If there is a problematic group then doing Circle Time can have a strong effect.

(Author, interview)

One trainer had used Circle Time with secondary age and sixth-form students:

Any school which takes PSHE seriously can't do it unless they do Circle Time, even secondary. More primaries have introduced PSHE. But investment in Circle Time means delivering the national curriculum, talking and listening, in the right environment.

(Trainer)

One trainer reported that a year 1 teacher was using group work techniques in the literacy hour, asking children to tell a partner about a problem and a success in their reading. Another school ran its school council on Circle Time lines.

A whole-school approach was said to 'make a big difference with respect to playground behaviour'. If Circle Time was integrated with other aspects of PSE and part of the school's whole approach it could influence school ethos and feed into the development of policies and practices.

Although writers and trainers generally acknowledged that Circle Time owed a good deal to what teachers brought to it and how teachers conducted it, few described benefits for teachers. One said 'Circle Time appeals fundamentally to teachers' belief systems and what drove them into teaching was a significant interest in values. Circle Time helps them to get the joy back into teaching.'

There did not appear to be any evidence from trainers about connections between use of Circle Time and the development of cognitive skills and achievements, although one trainer/writer remarked: 'if senior management keep an eye on Circle Time it can help academically. ... because the child's confidence also grows.'

One or two trainers mentioned they had asked teachers and children to evaluate their experiences of Circle Time. Teachers had been asked about any effects of Circle Time strategies on their teaching in general. There was a sense among one or two trainer/writers that some Circle Times could be managed and run by children themselves. There was general acknowledgement that Circle Time needed to be evaluated by schools and that teachers needed to review their practices for quality and coherence. One trainer expressed some concerns about the image of Circle Time. He wanted to promote better quality work on Circle Time. He expressed some anxiety about Circle Time 'taking off' and of 'blanket introduction' of Circle Time as a panacea. On the other hand, he also feared that Circle Time might be 'rejected before it has been tried', because of examples of bad practice.

2.2 Circle Time in policy and practice: schools' aims, training and provision

The research included telephone interviews with senior managers and key Circle Time teachers in a sample of 57 nursery, infant and junior schools which had previously identified themselves as using Circle Time (see Appendix 1).

2.2.1 Length of time Circle Time used

All schools reported still using Circle Time, except two very small rural schools with fewer than 70 pupils each. One of these schools had only used Circle Time a few times to improve behaviour and self-esteem with year 5–6. Teachers felt they learned more about the children but that the strategy 'loses its impact' because of small group size. However, the school was planning to reintroduce it. The other school had used Circle Time regularly over two or three years to foster support and respect in its mixed age (8–11 years) classes but felt that Circle Time might be 'inappropriate' as the younger children could not sustain confidentiality.

These two schools were excluded from further data analysis, which is based on 55 schools.

Thirty-one schools had started to use Circle Time within the last three years, whilst 14 had used it for five or more years, including School B (8 years) and School J (10 years).

Some teachers reported that 'Circle Time has always seemed to fit in with the way we teach. It has just naturally developed. We've always preferred to sit in a circle even before we had heard of "Circle Time". Circle Time has just formalised it and given it a name.' However, it could be questioned whether these teachers were implementing Circle Time according to the structures, rules and strategies recommended in the manuals.

2.2.2 Reasons for introducing Circle Time

Asked about the reason why they or the school started to use Circle Time, many respondents gave more than one answer. The categories derived from the reasons given are not commensurate (e.g. between 'behaviour' and 'training'), for they suggest different motivation, routes or varying stages of implementation. A difference also exists between those relatively few schools which mentioned 'formal' training as a catalyst and those whose staff had just observed others' practice.

Five schools said Circle Time was 'part of PSE/PSHE' and 14 claimed it was introduced 'to develop feelings', such as self-esteem (8) or 'to express feelings' (6). However, most schools had begun Circle Time for one or more of the following reasons:

- to meet pupils' needs

- to develop a range of skills (23), such as speaking (8), listening (8), social skills (5) or problem-solving skills (2)

  Initially we started to use it to develop speaking and listening skills. Everyone has a job within the circle, whether it is contributing or actively listening. We use Circle Time to develop self-esteem, and the rule of only being able to speak when they are holding the object works well as it gives children confidence as they know they won't be interrupted.

  (Key stage 1 coordinator)

- to improve behaviour, attitudes or relationships (23), either in response to behavioural problems (12) or to implement a behavioural policy or approach (11).

  The special needs coordinator in School D reported that Circle Time was introduced in response to behavioural and attitudinal problems, for instance when children made accusations about other children. With a specialist in Circle Time they had also used it with a whole year group (year 6 and 7). A discussion on children's reaction to the expulsion of a footballer before the World Cup enabled them to introduce the idea of team work and the effects of individual's non-cooperation.

- to develop, recognise and express feelings (14). A headteacher of an infant school with a written policy about Circle Time, as part of an approach to positive behaviour, with the aim to increase self-esteem and empathy said:

  > Circle Time gives children a chance to speak, though no one is forced to do so. We need to value their opinions and encourage them to be more caring and tolerant. Circle Time should contribute to the children's SMSC development and provide an opportunity for hopes and fears and feelings to be voiced in a safe and non-threatening environment. We need to create a calm, peaceful time for quiet thought and reflection in the hurly-burly way of life we have.
  >
  > (Infant school headteacher)

- as a result of training. This included: 'formal' training (13), 'informal' discussion (6), observing others' success (4), or by seeing books or resources (2)

  - informal training. Shadowing the PSHE coordinator in a previous school, one SEN coordinator had seen how Circle Time enabled 'difficult' children to discuss school rules 'in a civilised manner'

  - formal training. One small school started Circle Time after the head had attended several LEA courses in connection with its anti-bullying campaign, which included workshops on Circle Time as a method to increase self-esteem

  - elsewhere. An LEA adviser had conducted an INSET session on Circle Time for all staff, including lunchtime supervisors in an urban school (School K). The PSE coordinator and one or two staff started using it and then other staff began to see the benefits and followed suit

- to fit curriculum constraints or as part of planned PSE/PSHE (5 schools)

  The curriculum is so squeezed that it is very hard to fit PSHE in, especially with the pressures of the numeracy and literacy hour. So through having designated time for Circle Time we may cover some PSHE issues.

  (Headteacher of a JMI school)

- for the benefit of teachers. Only one school mentioned introducing Circle Time because there were some anxieties and antagonism at the time amongst certain staff in the school, especially in meetings. Circle Time helped in 'reinforcing the positives' and it enabled staff to 'overcome their differences'.

2.2.3 Aims

Respondents' were asked their aims for using Circle Time. Some gave more than one response. Aims fell into four main, somewhat overlapping, categories:

1. to develop communication skills (46), particularly listening skills (19), speaking skills (15) and talking about/sharing thoughts, feelings and ideas (7). For example, in one class children chair and lead Circle Time themselves according to a Circle Code. This enabled the teacher sometimes to observe the sessions and make an assessment of children's interpersonal abilities.

2. to develop individual pupils (37), increasing self-esteem (29), giving quieter children a chance to speak (4), talking about their own problems (3) and developing their identity (1)

3. to develop pupils socially (26), encouraging respect and tolerance for each other (10), encouraging turn taking (5), building up relationships and trust (4), creating a sense of belonging (4), developing social skills (2), helping children to empathise (1)

4. to improve behaviour (20), creating shared rules (11) and promoting problem solving (9).

Sometimes aims covered a mixture of these:

I wanted the children to learn to share and to respect each other. It also gives them help with socialising skills. We have a lot of children who

*can't sit and listen. Yes, it's the listening skills too, learning to respect
the points of view of others and that they may not always have the same
opinions.*

(Headteacher of an infant school)

One respondent said that her aims were different each week, depending on
what they discussed.

Some other school responses about aims included:

- pupil empowerment. Two schools used Circle Time to give children
  more influence over school organisation and life by preparing their
  school council meetings agenda or reporting back to the class and
  discussing issues. One proponent interviewed saw this as a way of
  giving pupils more control over the Circle Time sessions. The
  Woodcraft Folk use Circle Time to develop democratic skills and
  encourage members to participate democratically in activities

- pupil integration. One school, with a mobile population, used Circle
  Time to help children to settle in the school, to create 'a class culture'
  and as a team building activity

- conflict resolution. School K used Circle Time as a means of conflict
  resolution and to help children understand, empathise and deal with
  family or community incidents, for example, the public arrest of a
  parent.

The extent to which aims articulated by the respondents, mostly senior
managers, were shared by their colleagues depended on the number of
other staff who were regularly involved in Circle Time and whether the
school saw itself as having adopted a whole-school approach. One
headteacher's response summed this up: 'I like to think so. There are
nearly 20 staff, some are more committed than others.'

2.2.4 Training

The majority of respondents (47) had received training in how to use
Circle Time, of whom 30 could recall or date when training had taken
place. Twenty-three reported that their training had taken place within the
previous three years.

Cost was a factor, especially for small schools. Some schools reported
'There was a course but it could not be afforded as a lot of money is going

on literacy hour'; others considered the training offered by one proponent to be 'very expensive'. However, one respondent believed that formal training was not necessary; instead, teachers should discuss their experiences of Circle Time.

Respondents reported various forms of active training which included Circle Time, and occasionally they and/or their colleagues had experienced more than one type of training course. There was a broad range of sources of and deliverers of training – fellow teachers, support teams, LEAs and Circle Time proponents, in and out of school – which are difficult to categorise. There did not seem to be any geographical relationship to training, although some LEAs appeared to have been more proactive than others in offering training on Circle Time.

Types of training included:

- privately sponsored training in or out of school. Ten schools mentioned Jenny Mosley, who had conducted training in LEAs, with cluster schools and in individual schools. Many said this had been extremely useful, especially the practical aspects. One head had been on privately-run school council training, which included Circle Time as a method of involving all pupils. Another teacher had been inspired by university in-school training to undertake an MA in behaviour modification

- in-school training by LEA staff which included Circle Time was provided by the behavioural support unit (6 schools); LEA advisers/inspectors, especially for PSHE (4 schools) or English language; teachers from other schools (2) and the Education Psychological Service (1). These school-based training sessions might be a single meeting or occasionally a whole or half day

- within LEA training. Provision included: curriculum and learning support (4 schools) or creativity (1); courses on special education needs (4) and child protection (1); linked thematic courses including anti-bullying (4). These courses usually lasted a whole day or more, during which Circle Time had been included as a session or workshop.

Most teachers had no subsequent contact relevant to the training. In only a few cases was follow-up reported, but where this occurred and real links were established, the support was much appreciated.

Ten respondents cited resources as a form of, or addition to, training. Manuals by Jenny Mosley were predominantly mentioned, but some said they needed more time to read them. One head mentioned a BBC video about positive behaviour, rather than formal training. In addition to those sources indicated above, other schools mentioned first hearing about Circle Time through Kidscape, TACADE pack (Evans, 1990), Curry and Bromfield (1994) and Woodcraft Folk (1995).

When asked about the usefulness of training, 24 respondents gave a very general positive comment ('useful' or 'very useful'), which might suggest that they had not always had the chance to evaluate the training they received. Those who were more specific reported that the training had helped to:

- give more ideas/techniques (10 respondents)

- provide practical first-hand experience (5)

- give good follow-up (4)

- introduce teachers to Circle Time (4)

- model Circle Time and see how it was run (3)

- enable teachers to discuss ideas (3)

- introduce schools to more resources (3)

- show how Circle Time could be used across the curriculum (1).

Sometimes training came from several sources. The most appreciated training included personal experience of the strategy. Some key issues emerged.

- Clarify expectations. In School N the LEA adviser spent time eliciting the teachers' expectations of Circle Time, which teachers thought was important.

- Class observation. Observation of how Circle Time had successfully raised children's self-esteem in another school made staff keen to include it in their behaviour management strategies, as they had 'a lot of difficult children who find it hard to express themselves'. A trainer from the LEA EBD unit gave 'very useful' training which 'set out a clear framework and gave more ideas about using Circle Time ... provided an opportunity to discuss Circle Time as an aspect of positive behaviour management.'

- Research participation. A headteacher who experienced Circle Time in an LEA PSE course said it 'was useful as it gave teachers a chance to take part in a Circle Time session themselves. We all had to sit in a circle and pass a piece of paper round – we could only speak when we were holding it. However, this didn't work as we kept interrupting each other.'

- Several resource inputs. In one school some staff took part in a Circle Time session at an SEN coordinators' meeting and another member received in-house training from the Behavioural Support team. The school also had books from two proponents. All ten teachers in the school reported using Circle Time, seven of them consistently.

- Relevance to the class context. A member of the English Language Support staff showed videos to infant school staff and discussed how Circle Time could be used to develop language skills and self-esteem for speakers of English as a second language.

- Developing teacher confidence. In School G, a few teachers had attended a course on 'Self-esteem in Circle Time', led by an LEA educational psychologist, before implementing Circle Time in the nursery. This was followed up by a day's INSET from a headteacher on the methods used with success in her school. The staff hoped to observe Circle Time in use there.

One LEA trainer noted that the usefulness of training is related to its dissemination to school staff. In one school, the SEN coordinator had attended an LEA advisory course which provided a booklet of ideas for use in Circle Time. The SEN coordinator had 'cascaded' the knowledge to the class assistant, and then other teachers wanted to know more about it.

2.2.5 A whole-school approach to Circle Time

Some proponents emphasise that Circle Time must be embraced as a whole-school approach for it to be truly effective. For example, Mosley (1993a:44) provides an illustration of a whole-school self-esteem and positive behaviour policy cycle which covers the classroom, lunchroom and playground, and involves partnerships between teachers, lunch-time supervisors and parents. She describes a range of related activities such as 'golden rules', incentives and lunch-time practices and recommends inviting parents to watch Circle Time sessions.

When asked whether there was a whole-school approach to Circle Time, senior teachers often made a rather vague reference to PSHE. However, this did not necessarily indicate that Circle Time was a fully considered and integral part of their policy and practices. Most schools said that they used Circle Time as 'part of', or 'closely related to PSHE', without going into any further detail. For example:

> *Circle Time fits into PSHE. There used to be a whole-school approach, but there isn't any more, as there are too many demands from their curriculum areas. Circle Time isn't used consistently through the school, but by individual teachers. They can 'pick or choose' whether or not to use Circle Time.*
>
> (Senior nursery teacher, School G)

However, a few schools indicated that Circle Time was an integrated part of their practices and a strategy to attain some of their fundamental policy objectives. Two schools had written policies for specific aims and objectives.

School K had adopted a timetabled whole-school approach and was part of a larger 'Family Links' Scheme, which offered resources for a ten-week programme on Circle Time and support meetings to discuss progress. Teachers and pupils used a shared vocabulary in Circle Time.

Another school contacted in the telephone survey was extending Circle Time as part of a new PSE policy with more resources.

> *It is a whole-school policy, but how it is delivered is more or less up to individual teachers. There are three main areas. Firstly, 'Myself and getting to know you', then on to 'How to make friends', followed in the final term by 'Citizenship and community'.*

There are many factors which influence whether Circle Time becomes a whole-school approach (see Chapters 3 and 4), including:

- is there a 'top-down' approach led by the head and senior managers, perhaps as a way of addressing certain challenging issues (e.g. behaviour problems)?

- is there a 'bottom-up' approach, whereby the enthusiasm and commitment of an individual or a few teachers spreads and becomes a shared approach with common goals and a reasonably coherent set of practices?

- how significant are training and ongoing opportunities to focus on Circle Time?

- how much depends on the cohesiveness of the school and its staff?

- how influential are the leadership by the head and PSHE or SEN coordinator?

The number of staff in each school using Circle Time varied considerably, from a lone teacher to virtually the whole staff. Most commonly, two or three teachers made active and regular use of the strategy. Even where schools reported a whole-school approach (for example, School J), there quite often appeared to be one or two teachers who did not use it. Moreover, not all teachers within a school used the same approach or method. Some teachers reported regretting that they could not observe each other's Circle Time sessions. As a result, they were generally unsure of how other teachers in their school were using it and felt they all had their own slant.

Teachers and others need a good deal of commitment to make Circle Time successful as a whole-school approach. Our research findings suggest that there were limited opportunities in many schools for ongoing structured discussion about Circle Time practices, successes and failures and consequently that a whole-school approach to Circle Time is relatively rare.

Another aspect is the extent to which schools include their non-teaching staff, particularly lunch-time supervisors, non-teaching assistants and special needs assistants in Circle Time. Mosley argues that lunch-time supervisors should be included and even suggests dividing playgrounds up into separate areas of activity. One teacher felt that Circle Time was a tool for resolving problems, so should only be used by the teacher who knows the children well, as Circle Time can uncover sensitive issues which need to be dealt with seriously and with professionalism. Very few schools in our telephone survey mentioned that lunch-time supervisors were involved, although a few reported that they intended to involve lunch-time supervisors in training. In one school, the techniques used in Circle Time were passed on to the mid-day supervisors, for example, to try to ensure that each child gets listened to and gets a fair hearing. In School K, the lunch-time staff did Circle Time training alongside teachers.

Schools made no mention of including parents in Circle Time (see p. 112). It may be said that teachers are wary about including parents or simply do not see it as relevant.

To gain a fuller picture of whether Circle Time is included in a whole-school approach, we explored whether schools engaged in complementary activities such as 'golden rules', special stickers, lunch-time certificates, developing sanctions and 'mix-em up' games (Mosley, 1993b). A few schools indicated that they had adopted such approaches as part of a discipline policy supported by Circle Time.

In one primary school where Circle Time was partly used to raise self-esteem, the school held a 'special mention' assembly highlighting ideas mentioned in Circle Time, such as a child being especially kind. The child was then presented with a certificate saying why s/he is special or what s/he has done which is kind.

Classes involved and time allocated

In our sample, Circle Time was used with children in the Nursery (3 schools) up to year 7 (2 schools). There was no particular difference between the number of year groups involved overall. A few respondents had reservations about doing Circle Time with Nursery and Reception children, and one or two thought it was too late to introduce in year 7. Occasionally reasons for distinguishing usage between key stages were offered, for example:

- in School F Circle Time was used throughout key stage 1, partly with the idea of 'helping the classes to get together as a group, especially at the beginning of term'. But provision was also related to the fact that it was 'easier to timetable' for key stage 1 than for key stage 2

- in School M, Circle Time was used in the Nursery, Reception, year 1 and 2, but to a lesser extent in year 3. In year 5, children suggested some of the ideas to talk about during Circle Time. In year 6 the geographical arrangement of the classroom made it difficult for children to sit around in the circle, but they had been splitting into groups to discuss and debate topics. A group representative was then nominated to put forward the group's ideas. The rest of the class had to listen before intervening.

Circle Time was mostly used in whole class groups by the class teacher, but occasionally it was conducted by a PSE or SEN coordinator. Sometimes a teacher, such as a Section 11 teacher, would take a small group of children for Circle Time: 'It gives them a time when they know they are going to be listened to.'

Most teachers used Circle Time for between 20–30 minutes per week, although sessions for younger children might be shortened (around 15 minutes), as appropriate for their developmental level and attention span. Curry and Bromfield (1994) suggest that shorter and more frequent sessions are more successful. Generally respondents indicated that teachers used Circle Time as and when they felt it was needed, sometimes in addition to a timetabled session. Some teachers were concerned that if Circle Time was used too often, the children would become bored with it and it would not be as effective. Others thought it was rather a special 'personal time' for the teacher and her class: 'It gives children a sense of belonging to a family.' Whether or not Circle Time was timetabled sometimes varied from class to class within a school. The timing of Circle Time may be as important as the fact that it is timetabled (see p. 77).

2.2.6 Provision

Responses to 'How is Circle Time used?' fell into three main categories (respondents may have given more than one answer).

1. Activities. These included: games (12 schools); passing an object around (5); role play/drama (3); music (2); story time (2); puppets (1); 'children show things' (1).

2. Content. Topics included curriculum subjects (7 schools), rules (4) and 'sharing news' (3). Topics were chosen by teachers (9 schools), pupils (10) or through a confidential suggestion box (2).

3. Timing. In 28 schools respondents used Circle Time specifically in response to or to discuss playground behaviour or bullying problems. In 13 other schools it was allocated a time usually weekly, quite often after playtime or lunchtime. In nine schools Circle Time was used spontaneously. Indications were that Circle Time was often used 'later in the week, because the class builds up and there is a kind of buzz' (School N). However, a few schools had discovered that Friday afternoon was not the best time as 'children are excited and tired'.

A few schools mentioned specific incidents which had led to their using Circle Time to good effect:

- the parents of a profoundly deaf child claimed that he had experienced bullying. Circle Time was used to talk this through and to address wider issues of disability

- in an infant school, Circle Time often followed an incident reported by a mid-day assistant, such as a child being unkind or throwing something at another child. This might be followed up by a general discussion about playgrounds.

Some teachers described in detail how they used Circle Time, for example, an infant teacher who had used Circle Time for five years said:

I personally have a fairly set format with my class of 26. We usually start with a warm up game, for example 'Hot potato', which is fairly quick. Then in the middle we might go round and all say something. Finally we may finish with another game. Recently we have actually come out of the circle and discussed issues in smaller groups with a nominated scribe. We then get together in the circle and bring everyone's ideas together. I have an allotted time each week. I generally raise issues, as I haven't yet had a child ask me to discuss something. If that did happen, we would probably address it then in a discussion. But I would probably also approach it again in the allotted Circle Time session.

The head of an inner city infant school described how Circle Time had shifted from exploring a planned topic to being used less regularly, generally to deal with poor behaviour, or if a child had had a difficult time. For example, there has been some use of Circle Time to help refugee children articulate their experiences and to enable others to empathise with them: 'We have to take the lead from the children, whether they want to talk about their experiences or not, it's up to them.'

A reception teacher had two different ways of using Circle Time:

Firstly, I used it as we had a few children for whom English was their second language. We used it first thing in the morning everyday and called it 'news' rather than Circle Time. This helps with their speaking, listening and questioning skills. Secondly we used it once a week with a teacher of English as a second language to try to build up self-esteem and introduce them to turn-taking.

39

An acting head described Circle Time as 'a calming activity' which was used to 'set another activity off'. Music was a strong feature of Circle Time. For example, she played a song called 'Heaven' and then the children talked about their concept of heaven. Circle Time was seen as a sensitive forum for discussing such ideas. A black teacher had read a story about black and white animals fighting with each other to introduce the concept of racism and make the children more aware. As a result children had learnt that the school took bullying and racism very seriously.

Respondents were quite eager to talk in some detail about and discuss the games and activities used, such as Salad Bowl (friendship mixing), Wink Murders (getting to know other children) and Special Person/Child of the Day. A few schools mentioned conducting Parachute Games requiring cooperation to achieve the task. By contrast, few schools outlined a clear structure or order of activities and some were open about not passing an object around the circle. Some schools appeared to follow a set format and procedures. Occasionally these were quite complicated. One school conducted a carousel, one circle inside another. Another did mini-Circle Time with a friendship group if problems occurred in the playground.

The National Curriculum and cross-curricular links

Some proponents have been at pains to stress that Circle Time 'meets specific requirements for the English National Curriculum' (Mosley, 1996:240–3; see also Curry and Bromfield, 1994:8) and to provide quite explicit descriptions of how to achieve this. Some proponents (see pp. 23) have argued that Circle Time is a 'teaching method' which should be used as such.

Some schools mentioned using different curriculum areas or topics or using Circle Time in a range of different curriculum areas:

- to 'talk about special places and feelings' in history and in PSE

- to discuss philosophical topics in RE (2 schools)

- to develop speaking and listening skills as part of the English curriculum

- to play maths games

- to discuss controversial issues in science such as experiments on animals, and in history as a forum for debate

- where Circle Time fitted with PSE, sessions were often held before drama

- to discuss PSHE topics such as healthy eating

- to contribute to an anti-drugs initiative

- to develop a shared vocabulary in Circle Time e.g. 'warm fuzzy' and 'cold prickly' feelings (see Curry and Bromfield, 1994:70–3), followed up with art activities and collages for the two types of feelings. The school was planning to introduce parents to this shared vocabulary

- to discuss environmental issues

- to evaluate and recollect earlier work. Link each pupil contributing something learnt earlier in a curriculum subject.

By contrast, some respondents saw Circle Time very much in isolation from, or in competition with, the National Curriculum: 'We need uninterrupted time ... we would like to use it every day, but can't because of the curriculum'; 'We would like Circle Time to have a proper slot in the curriculum'; 'There is not enough time in the curriculum for Circle Time.'

The introduction of the literacy and numeracy hours were highlighted as competing with time for Circle Time. Some schools felt that they would need to become more flexible with their use of Circle Time. Interestingly, one school mentioned the possibility of including Circle Time in the literacy hour. Another school mentioned that staff had not been able to attend a Circle Time training course as money had to be spent training for the literacy hour.

2.2.7 Outcomes

We explored schools' claims for the effects of Circle Time in three main respects: learning outcomes for pupils, learning by teachers and wider effects on the school.

Pupils' learning

First, and most importantly, we wanted to know what learning outcomes headteachers and others identified for pupils. Responses fell into three main categories.

1.   Communication skills. The main skills identified were: talking about and sharing thoughts, feelings and ideas (11 schools); improving

41

listening skills (10); improving speaking skills, including in English as a second language (6); learning to take turns (4).

2.   Personal development. Respondents reported considerable personal self-enhancement for some pupils, especially increased self-esteem and self-confidence (17 schools); quieter children having a chance to speak (16); facilitating reflection on behaviour (1).

3.   Social development. Circle Time also enabled the improvement of pupils' social skills, attitudes and behaviour, 'the tools of personality', such as: encouraging respect or tolerance for each other and one another's feelings (12 schools); promoting problem-solving skills and improving behaviour (7); feeling a sense of belonging in the class (5); developing social skills (3); encouraging empathy (2); creating shared values or rules (2); building up relationships and trust (1).

The main effects of Circle Time on pupils were claimed to be increasing self-esteem, encouraging respect, sharing feelings, and enabling quiet children to speak. As one senior teacher in the survey acknowledged:

Self-esteem definitely increases as they feel valued and they are not laughed at or commented on. They all have their 15 seconds of fame! Their listening and cooperation skills increase, as there is no butting-in, instead there is turn taking.

Teachers had generally not undertaken any serious evaluation or standardised assessment of children's personal and social development. But some specific examples are worthy of mention.

•   One teacher mentioned that when one boy joined the school, his mother told her that he was a 'bit strange'. The teacher described seeing him in the playground on his own. When she approached him he said he did not want to play with anyone. The mother and teacher drew up an action plan which included Circle Time. Half way through the term the boy had begun to mix with a small group of pupils. By the end of the year, he participated fully in Circle Time and also joined in with other children at break time. His mother said this change had also been evident at home.

•   A teacher at one infants school described the fact that one pupil spoke in Circle Time as a 'monumental occasion'. Another noted that children were more confident in role play and to talk in assembly. One girl, who did not usually speak put her hand up and used the word 'intimidated', which had surprised the head.

- Many schools surveyed mentioned that Circle Time gave children the chance to express their own feelings and ideas and listen to the feelings of others. The deputy head in School H went a stage further, claiming that they felt it had extended and broadened the children's thinking.

- One telephoned school considered that Circle Time conferred benefits in that it enabled children to talk with children beyond their normal friendship groups:

  It helps children to think of others' feelings and empathise. It helps them become aware of the consequences of their actions and 'opens their eyes' to the circumstances of others. It gives them a greater awareness as often they think 'that sort of thing doesn't happen in my family'.

- One teacher said:

  I find the children are very enthusiastic about Circle Time, even the year 6 ... They like the rules of anonymity. They learn about the philosophy of being positive. They learn how to be critical in a positive way. They also realise that they can say something nice about someone and not be embarrassed. It's up to the teacher to make sure they are sincere and honest.

- The sense of a group and community was emphasised by some schools surveyed: 'It gels the class. This is especially important with the way our classes work, that is it helps introduce the two different years in one class.'

- Circle Time could also allow all pupils to have a voice: 'It enables all pupils to feel equal and have a say, not just the most dominant. It encourages children to respect each other.' (School G).

On further analysis it was found that, in some cases, there was a poor correlation between respondents' main aims for Circle Time with the outcomes they identified. Some categories which scored highly as 'aims' seemed to score lower as 'outcomes' and vice versa. For example, 19 respondents saw improving listening skills as an aim of Circle Time, while only ten reported their improvement as an outcome.

Conversely, only four schools set out to give quieter children the chance to speak, whereas 16 saw it as an outcome. But in some cases there was greater correlation between reported aims and pupil outcomes, for example with encouraging turn-taking, building up relationships, creating a sense of belonging, helping children empathise, and developing social skills.

What does this gap in perceptions mean? Were teachers surprised at the outcomes? Have teachers and schools given themselves opportunities to examine their intentions for Circle Time and evaluate their perceived outcomes from it? Is there a gap between what senior managers intend when a school engages in Circle Time and what they hear back from teachers as to its effects?

Outcomes for teachers

When asked what they themselves had learned from Circle Time, teachers' and senior managers' responses fell into two main categories: learning about children and learning about teaching.

- Learning about children. The largest single category of responses was to the effect that they had got to know the children better (21 schools). A typical response was: 'I feel you gain an insight into the children and see what really makes them tick.' Conversely, one respondent also thought that 'children get to know me better'. Teachers had also learned to value each child as an individual (13). Others had found that 'Children surprise you' or 'Suddenly the quiet ones speak' (6). Four schools noted that children were more expressive, sharing ideas or 'confide in you'.

- Learning about teaching. Thirteen schools mentioned that teachers had become more self-aware in their teaching and had learnt more about how to listen, ask questions and 'take a back seat'. Three schools mentioned the need to be aware of sensitive issues and disclosures. One respondent noted that Circle Time helps work on PSE and another that it 'leads to more open teaching':

> *Oh lots! Patience. How deep children's personalities are. How precious individuality is. The importance of respecting them, shutting up and letting them talk, not just whipping through the curriculum. You become more than a teacher because in Circle Time you do what they do. If they sit on the floor, then I sit on the floor. It's a whole new approach to communicating with them, as there is no judging, no 'That's good' or 'That's bad'. It's just talking.*
>
> (Key stage 1 coordinator)

Respondents sometimes mentioned what they perceived as the significance of the fact that they were sitting at the same level as the children, whether it was on a chair or on the floor, to minimise an 'us' and 'them' situation (c.f. the 'Quality Circles' used in industry, Dawson and McNess, 1998:2). Many teachers commented that Circle Time gives them the chance to temporarily lose the 'teacher' relationship, and take on a new role: 'Everyone has a chance to be equal, even though I'm the teacher. It takes you out of your teacher role and more into a friend or a big brother/sister role'. Another teacher felt that the children knew her 'as a person now, not just a teacher'. When teachers adopt what Mosley describes as a 'facilitative' role, it may be that children become more responsive, which, in turn, helps teachers to know children better:

> Circle Time gives the children more power. For some teachers this may be a problem. Although the teacher is still there she takes a back seat and becomes one of the group. So she loses a degree of power and control. Those who you think are quite insensitive suddenly come out and say something which totally changes your opinion. You see another side of their personality.
>
> (Special needs teacher, School D)

Another school had found that children said things in Circle Time which they would not say in other circumstances. Teachers suggested this might be due to the trust existing in the circle. A headteacher in a middle class area where 'children usually articulate the desired views' said that he had learnt that the children were more knowledgeable about certain subjects, such as drugs and animal welfare, than he would have thought. Some teachers mentioned that because of Circle Time they had become more aware of the problems which their pupils faced.

The senior staff who mainly responded in the telephone interview gave interesting answers as to what they had learned, but they often needed prompting. This suggests that they are not fully aware of how they benefit from Circle Time as teachers and in the teaching and learning process. As with all pedagogical strategies, teachers need opportunities as individuals and as a whole staff to reflect on their learning. However, only a handful of respondents seemed to have observed (rather than conducted) Circle Time sessions.

Wider school effects
We were interested to know if Circle Time, advocated by some as part of a whole-school process, had any identifiable effects on the school. Respondents often said that it was hard to pinpoint changes as being due

just to Circle Time, especially when not all teachers were using it. This tends to reinforce our impression that most schools were not using Circle Time in a systematic or cohesive way as a whole-school approach to teaching and learning, which they could reflect upon in terms of clear and distinct institutional aims and outcomes.

Nevertheless, several respondents claimed that Circle Time had become an important learning strategy and had improved the schools' ethos. Research on Circle Time in Wiltshire supported this (Dawson and McNess, 1998).

- One school mentioned that Circle Time contributed to its peaceful ethos and another described that it gave the whole school the chance to be quiet, as Circle Time was timetabled at the same time.

- The headteacher of School I claimed that the effects of Circle Time were 'gradually filtering through the school'. In particular the children in the top year were calmer and more tolerant, waiting their turn for attention.

- The head of School K claimed that in a school where there were 'a lot of conflicts, explosions and crises in school and families at war, Circle Time gives children a vocabulary to talk things through, instead of using their fists.' She said that it resulted in 'more rounded individuals' and a 'calmer' atmosphere in school.

The head who said 'The use of Circle Time has been part of a bigger push towards improving behaviour, in which there have been noticeable differences' might have spoken for many respondents.

2.2.8 Issues

During the telephone interviews respondents spontaneously and incidentally mentioned several issues which they had encountered when using Circle Time. These are outlined below, and served as hypotheses to be tested in the case-study school-based research encounters (see Chapters 3 and 4).

Different definitions and understanding of Circle Time
The definition and implementation of 'Circle Time' vary between schools, in terms of: purpose, timing and age of pupils involved, as well as how it

is used and the type of resources. Some schools appeared unaware of basic concepts of Circle Time, such as sitting in a circle, at the same level and passing an object. On the other hand, a few respondents said that when the children sat in a circle, they knew that they had to take turns and so they no longer passed around an object. Some teachers have adapted the Circle Time method of organisations, such as Woodcraft Folk, in their classrooms. The diversity in interpretation and practice between and within schools (possibly arising from lack of planning or training) makes comparisons difficult (see Lang, 1998).

A particular issue was whether the use of Circle Time is seen as therapy. Proponents' and trainers' views differ. Whilst Mosley endorses this approach for small groups of troubled children who are 'beyond' responding to normal motivational strategies (1993b:38–9), an LEA trainer insisted that Circle Time should not be used to explore deeply psychological issues or individual casework. However, understandings of 'therapy' also differ. One school described discussing 'food and lunches as there was a girl who was not eating properly'. Is this 'therapeutic'? And should Circle Time be used in this way?

Practical organisation

Some respondents raised practical issues. The general consensus was that a suitable space was needed for Circle Time and most classrooms could not provide this, particularly for classes exceeding 30. Some classes seemed to resort to discussions in smaller groups instead of in a circle, an approach supported by Curry and Bromfield (1994), who suggest 20 as the ideal size for a Circle Time group. Some classes use a carpeted area in the classroom or elsewhere (e.g. TV room). Whilst the school hall offers more space for laying out chairs or playing games, it could result in less privacy.

Many respondents pointed out the importance of being in a perfect circle, because they felt the children lost interest if eye contact was not maintained. Some disruption occurred when playing games that involved the children swapping places and especially if children sat on the floor, it was hard for them to return to an appropriate place and maintain the circle.

Learning to take turns and listen to each other was usually seen as a 'teething' problem. However, one head noted that although some of the quieter children 'open up, some of the statemented boys can get quite silly during Circle Time'.

47

Sensitivity, disclosure, confidentiality

Since the very nature of Circle Time and its environment and atmosphere is likely to engender a sense of belonging, it 'provides a forum for children to discuss sensitive issues that may be difficult to talk about in other situations'. A school in a deprived area reported that 'difficulties at home may get in the way of learning' and saw Circle Time as a chance to 'put down some baggage'.

Such disclosures can be challenging to manage and teachers need to consider carefully how such cases are best dealt with in a group and to follow a common procedure. This may be particularly so with child protection issues. When one girl said 'I don't like it when uncle touches me', the teacher replied 'Yes, it's horrible being tickled isn't it', and followed the matter through after the session. A few respondents called the one-to-one follow-up process 'Bubble Time'.

Myers (1998) stresses the importance of considering the sensitivity of themes, approaches and their follow up 'to promote positive experiences for both children and adults taking part in Circle Time' (Myers, 1998:35), but the literature generally appears to pay little attention to sensitivity. Only one telephone respondent mentioned that training had dealt with sensitive matters, pointing out that:

> *It was good as it helped teachers to become aware of when to show sensitivity with regard to feelings about controversial issues, for example drugs. It showed us when to tread carefully.*

Teachers who are insensitive, or who place pressure on a child to speak or talk about something they find frightening, might cause further stress for the child. One teacher said that staff were very aware of not prying and that they would not use Circle Time at sensitive times, if they knew a child was 'undergoing a traumatic experience'.

Curry and Bromfield (1998:15) see confidentiality as an essential requirement of the contract which needs to be developed within the Circle Time group. This was reiterated by one or two survey respondents. One of the two schools which had stopped using Circle Time, had done so because the younger children in their vertically grouped classes would not 'be able to keep quiet about what we talk about'.

Passing

The issue of whether or not children should be allowed to 'pass' also resulted in different practices. Most respondents gave children the chance to 'pass' if they did not want to speak. A few noted that it was usually the quiet or 'difficult' children who 'passed'. However, a university-based trainer proposed that 'passing' should be interpreted as 'thinking time', which means 'we will come back to you'. Is it an intrusion into the child's privacy to insist on a verbal contribution from a child who still does not want to speak after 'thinking time'?

Another respondent reported a slightly different example of an over enthusiastic child who wanted to conduct Circle Time. He let the children give each other stars, but by the end of the day the children were all arguing about who had given or not given them stars. The teacher mentioned it as an example of what may happen if activities are not properly thought through.

2.2.9 Future plans

All schools which were currently using Circle Time said they would continue to use it the following term, although some anticipated that the literacy and numeracy hour might affect how it was used. Plans to develop Circle Time practices included:

- choosing a new theme, 'probably cooperation, as they will be making new friends'

- developing Circle Time into a whole-school policy and using it more regularly, starting with year 1 and progressing through the school

- considering Circle Time as part of behavioural policy and hoping to develop a whole-school approach

- developing a written policy which includes Circle Time

- reviewing, monitoring or evaluating Circle Time

- training new staff in Circle Time, evaluating it and involving parents

- dedicating time on Friday mornings for the whole school to conduct Circle Time.

2.3 Key findings and issues

The telephone and face-to-face interviews with writers/trainers and senior school staff revealed the following:

◆ Circle Time has origins in humanistic psychology, groupwork, democratic processes and student-centred learning

◆ trainers expressed reservations about the lack of follow-up to training and the importance of dissemination to achieve a 'whole-school approach'. Other key concerns focused on the characteristics and role of the teacher in facilitating Circle Time and the responses of some pupils

◆ trainers identified benefits for pupils and schools, such as improvements to self-esteem and behaviour, communication, caring and school ethos. They recognised, however, the need to provide more evidence about the relationship of Circle Time to enhancing academic ability and the need for evaluation and review of the use of the strategy in school

◆ over half of the 55 schools sampled had used Circle Time for up to three years and some for as long as ten years. They had started to do Circle Time, sometimes as part of PSE and to develop children's feelings, but mostly to develop communication skills, improve behaviour, attitudes and relationships, or as a result of training. Examples are given of the predominantly pupil-oriented reasons school had for introducing Circle Time

◆ schools' main aims were to develop communication skills, enhance pupils' self-esteem or self-confidence and improve their social skills and behaviour. Sometimes they had several aims.

◆ the majority of interviewees had had some training, mostly within the previous three years. They had experienced a broad range of training sources and providers, in and out of school. However, there had been little follow-up and some teachers had implemented Circle Time on the basis of reading resource books only. Those who had training responded positively regarding its usefulness, especially when it gave them personal experience of participating in the circle

- the overall impression was of a lack of an integrated, cohesive and inclusive whole-school approaches to Circle Time. In most schools Circle Time was undertaken by only two or three class teachers who were not always aware of each other's practices. Classes from Nursery to year 6 did Circle Time, usually for 20–30 minutes weekly or 15 minutes for younger children

- Circle Time involved a range of activities and in around a quarter of schools children were able to raise their own issues. Circle Time was used spontaneously and sometimes timetabled, often after break or lunch times

- important learning outcomes for pupils related to communication, such as sharing feelings and listening, improving self-esteem and confidence, developing social skills, such as respect, problem solving and having a sense of belonging

- teachers also reported getting to know children better and learning about their own teaching, with greater awareness of their teaching style, of the need to listen and to begin to change their role

- there was not always a good correlation between respondents' stated aims and reported outcomes. Challenging issues and ethical concerns were raised

- most respondents found it difficult to identify wider school effects, but some claimed improved school ethos and behaviour

- most schools intended to continue using Circle Time and some had plans for new developments.

3 Primary teachers' perspectives and practices

The literature review and responses from proponents and headteachers have revealed many aims for introducing Circle Time into primary practice. This chapter focuses on responses from the class teachers who undertook Circle Time on a regular basis: their aims and their understanding of the values, attitudes, personal qualities, skills, dispositions or behaviour identified as the goals of Circle Time. For example, what do teachers count as self-esteem and how is it promoted? What main models of Circle Time do teachers use to implement the strategy?

3.1 Class teachers' aims

Headteachers' and teachers' aims in using Circle Time may vary between and within schools and classes and over time, depending on and in response to circumstances. Moreover, individual teachers may have a mix of aims and objectives, as this interviewee remarked:

> *I have several aims. I use it for getting to know the pupils as it's an opportunity to talk in a non-threatening way. We deal with issues there's not time to talk about at other times. And I also raise issues I'm aware about from what's happening with them, anything that might be affecting their class work or their well being.*

> (Year 5 teacher in School M)

In order to obtain an overall view, 28 primary teachers (nursery to year 6) were asked to choose up to three aims, in order of priority, from those reported in the available literature:

1. to help with problem solving (conflict resolution)

2. to encourage pupils to respect themselves and others

3. to create shared rules (and acceptance of them) and a code of behaviour

4. to develop communication, especially speaking and listening skills

5. to help children become more reflective and clearer about their own values

6. to encourage responsibility

7. to foster self-esteem and self-confidence in pupils

8. to develop trust

9. to encourage the sharing of thoughts and feelings

10. to develop a cooperative class (school) ethos

11. other.

Twenty-two of the 28 teachers indicated their aims and prioritised their responses. As their top priority aim, teachers chose 'to foster self-esteem and self-confidence in pupils' (10 teachers), 'to encourage pupils to respect themselves and others' (5) 'to develop communication, especially speaking and listening skills' (3), 'to encourage the sharing of thoughts and feelings' (2) and 'to help with problem solving (conflict resolution)' and 'to develop a cooperative class (school) ethos' (1 teacher each).

The overall ranking of aims selected by the teachers reiterated this pattern. The aim 'to foster self-esteem and self-confidence in pupils' received most choices (17), closely followed by 'to encourage pupils to respect themselves and others' (14) and 'to develop communication, especially speaking and listening skills' (11). These three aims accounted for 42 of the 66 selections. They also corresponded with the overall aims (though not ranking) of senior managers, who responded in the telephone survey. Another group of aims, which each received mention by six or seven teachers, were 'to help with problem solving (conflict resolution)', 'to develop a cooperative class (school) ethos' and 'to encourage the sharing of thoughts and feelings'. Other aims barely received acknowledgement. There was no clear pattern as to the choices of teachers according to their year group.

3.1.1 Putting aims into practice

In conversation, teachers elaborated on and gave examples of how they put their aims into practice.

- To help with problem solving (conflict resolution): Circle Time seemed to be widely used to sort out behavioural problems, including teasing, picking on someone or bullying.

Usually we talk about people's troubles in the playground and that. ... And [the teacher] *says that Circle Time is very important to tell everyone your problems. We have to try and sort out all your problems.*

(Year 4 girl, School I)

- To encourage pupils to respect themselves and others: Circle Time is sometimes used to celebrate achievements. For example, in one school pupils were allowed to bring dancing boots and swimming medals for a 'Show and Tell' round. 'They are allowed to congratulate each other and themselves in Circle Time and I encourage this sometimes' (year 5 teacher, School B).

- To create shared rules (and acceptance of them) and a code of behaviour: used as a whole-class activity, especially at the beginning of term (School K).

- To develop communication, especially speaking and listening skills: for quiet and inexpressive children, boisterous children and those children with English as an additional language.

- To help children become more reflective and clearer about their own values: in School H, which received Travelling children, Circle Time had been a useful strategy for exploring diversity in family values.

- To encourage responsibility: one school was planning to ask year 5 and 6 children their ideas of what to discuss in Circle Time: 'This gives the children a level of responsibility.' (Deputy Head, School H).

- To foster self-esteem and self-confidence in pupils:

  My long-term aim is to build self-esteem, showing them that all their opinions are valued and that they all have the right to say something and to be listened to. And on a more basic level I think it helps them with things like taking turns and listening to each other. The self-esteem is the long-term thing that hopefully, if it progresses through the school, it helps to build it up. But I don't think you do it that quickly.

  (Year 2/3 teacher, School B)

- To develop trust: in School J, where Circle Time was well established, staff were using it to develop progression in PSE. The school focused on building up trust among pupils through physical contact activities in which the child needs to trust a partner.

- To encourage the sharing of thoughts and feelings: one teacher,

  'searching for a way forward for this class [which] ...had a bad reputation' found that Circle Time linked with issues and processes, not curriculum content. It was helpful in an area where 'pupils' families do not enjoy much success' to 'probe behaviour and attitudes, such as aspirations and social attitudes, if issues come up when we are talking'.

  (Year 6 teacher, School N)

- To develop a cooperative class (school) ethos:

  Sometimes I may feel I need to use it to pull the class together. ...The main function is to keep everyone on an even keel and respect each other's ideas and privacy. It makes the class get on and iron out getting to know each other and sort out problems.

  (Year 5 teacher, School B)

3.2 Doing Circle Time

Many teachers have argued that the primary curriculum is overcrowded and over-prescriptive. What then motivates teachers to find a place for a learning strategy such as Circle Time? How does it fit with goals and curricula for PSE and Citizenship Education?

This section draws on observation and interviews with teachers and pupils to exemplify different models of provision for Circle Time. The observed sessions are described in some detail so as to convey the atmosphere, content and process of the experiences and to enable readers to ask their own critical questions and make their own appraisal.

3.2.1 Making provision for Circle Time

This section considers several ways of conducting Circle Time and identifies curriculum and delivery links which were made.

An integrated approach

One teacher had integrated Circle Time into her everyday practices, using it spontaneously to deal with a problem or conflict (e.g. playground behaviour, or when something was stolen) or to show something to the pupils. It was also used in music (taking turns with an instrument), drama (putting the actors in the middle) and story time (good for making eye contact). When a child with a disability joined the class, they discussed how they should treat people with disabilities and emphasised the need to maintain respect. The teacher needed to take special care of one insecure child and she asked the other children how they felt about this – whether they were jealous or in Circle Time felt they were not being given enough attention.

(Nursery teacher, School N)

A timetabled mixed ability approach

A teacher who ran a language department for children with special needs (autistic/dispraxic children) used Circle Time 'as a regular means of communication ... to help children feel comfortable about expressing themselves'. She timetabled mixed small (10–12) groups in which half the children had special needs. The children were encouraged to bring questions on their interests to the groups. There were three main rules: 'don't interrupt, sit as straight as possible and don't get upset.' At the end of the session, to develop memory skills, children tried to remember the subject about which each child had asked a question. The teacher congratulated those who did well.

(School B)

The inclusion of pupils with emotional and behavioural difficulties (EBD) in Circle Time was a controversial issue within schools.

A 'PSE' approach

A teacher in School F linked Circle Time with year 1 and 2 PSE work.

Exploring feelings

They will usually talk about their feelings. They have a suggestion box in the classroom – children can write down things that have made them sad, or nice things that have happened to them on a piece of paper and put it in the suggestion box. They can then talk about these things during Circle Time, with the emphasis being on anonymity. Exploring sad and happy feelings also links in with the work they do in PSE. They do a 'salad bowl' game where the children swap places and sit next to someone they don't know (e.g. 'those with green eyes change places'). Often they talk about what kind of things they have done at home, at the weekend or during school holidays. They also have question and answer sessions (e.g. children bring in pictures of pets and other children ask questions about them).

At the end of the summer term, in Circle Time with a group of 31 year 1 and 2 pupils, the teacher wanted to encourage a discussion of children's feelings about changing classes, as some were moving on. Many pupils claimed they were scared about going into a new class. In the second round the teacher then asked them to shut their eyes and think of the start of the previous school year and how they had felt. Then she suggested that they speak about what they had particularly enjoyed doing during the year. In this way she enabled them through their reflections to allay their own fears, as they had already experienced a moving on process. The teacher concluded the Circle Time positively by complimenting the class: 'I've enjoyed having such a grown-up sensible class. I've been able to write lovely reports about everyone, and you are all very hardworking.'

In School J, where Circle Time was long established, it became possible to have a more diverse, structured and developmental approach. Circle Time was used in various ways throughout the school: as a 'coming together time' at the end of the day (Reception); in the morning (year 2) and in response to problems or playground incidents, often at the request of children (year 6). In most classes Circle Time took place for half an hour weekly, but flexibly as organised by the teacher. According to the headteacher, it was seen as 'a secure environment which gives the children a chance to calm down and have their say'. The school was developing the idea of progression and assessment in PSE, with Circle Time activities as an integral part.

In School K where Circle Time was 'part of the whole PSE approach and is intrinsic to what we do', there was a common pattern of use: 'On Monday we discuss their weekend. Wednesday we have Child of the Day. Friday we talk about what was their favourite thing during the week.' Since the school had support from a local link project it had been 'necessary to plan quite carefully for the sessions'.

Small group work
In some schools, with additional classroom support, it was sometimes possible to undertake Circle Time in small groups. This was especially useful in a Nursery or Reception class, as in School K.

Warm and fuzzy

There were four girls and five boys in this small nursery group with a teacher and class assistant. In order to get them to sit in circle the teacher asked them to hold hands in a circle, then they all sat down. This resulted in a near perfect circle, especially as the group was small. The teacher was obviously very familiar to the children and well liked by them.

The teacher introduced a puppet, 'Mickey the Monkey', at the very beginning of the session and placed him on the desk behind her. At this introduction the children became excited and chatty, but the teacher gently reminded the children not to speak and they responded.

She explained that she had something in a plastic bag which she wanted them to feel and say how it felt. She did it first and said 'it feels all soft and warm'. Then she passed the bag around circle and all the children contributed.

Throughout, the teacher commented on what the children said, for example, 'Oh that's interesting'. The children found the activity quite amusing and laughed at some of each other's responses, such as 'Oh it's tickly'. Whilst they did listen well to each other, they sometimes had to be reminded that it was Circle Time and they had to be sensible.

When the object, a feather boa in a plastic bag, had gone round the whole circle the teacher explained that, how the feather boa felt was how they might feel if someone was kind to them. 'It's a warm, fuzzy feeling' she said, and the children echoed her, obviously already knowing the phrase. A child asked about 'cold and prickly' and the teacher said they were discussing that the next day. The teacher then took the boa round the circle and put it next to their faces. The children loved this.

Next the teacher rolled a small soft ball to a child who then had to say how it could make someone feel 'warm and fuzzy'. The first child failed to respond, so the teacher gave an answer and he agreed. One child said, 'I could give X a pinch, but no I'll give her a hug.' All the children put their hands up to have the ball rolled to them. The teacher tried to relate what pupils said to what was happening in the playground, for example 'Yes, we share the bikes outside don't we.' The children liked the 'warm fuzzy' terminology. Even after fifteen minutes, they were still attentive.

Then the teacher said they would have a story. The children eagerly moved, quickly and quietly, from the circle to look at the teacher as she read. After the story each child took a turn to stand up with the teacher and puppet, 'Mickey the Monkey'. The child then had to say something nice to another child. The teacher asked them to say something to make someone feel 'warm and fuzzy'. She told them it was 'all about compliments'. After this they got back in a circle to say goodbye. The teacher asked them to sit quietly, which they did, thanked them for their comments and asked them to see if they could continue this kind behaviour in the playground. They then went round the circle gently patting each other's shoulder and saying 'Goodbye'.

Involving other adults

Class teachers were usually prepared or happy to involve others in their Circle Time experiences, preferring participants to observers. The adults other than teachers involved were mostly teaching assistants or special needs assistants. However, they could also be somewhat sidelined. For example, in Reception/year1 in School F, the teaching assistant was in the classroom, tidying up. Although she could hear what was being said, she could not participate. Her exclusion from the Circle Time would have given messages about her role and status to the pupils. Even though the teaching assistant might be part of the circle, she might or might not contribute. We did not see constructive involvement of adults other than teachers in Circle Time sessions.

Making curriculum links
PSHE

Some teachers made specific links between Circle Time and other areas of experience, usually with PSHE or RE (see p. 40).

> *Often children will bring a model they have made in art lessons to Circle Time sessions to show the other children. ... And they talk about issues covered in PSE during Circle Time lessons.*
>
> (Year 1/2 teacher, School F)

Art

Similarly, a year 2 teacher (School M) said

> *It often links in with Art work. Circle Time sessions are used for 'Showing and Telling' where children bring along items from home or things they have drawn or made in class.... Circle Time sessions can be used for constructive criticism on Art work ... . Often the children bring in pictures which evoke feelings, they talk about how they feel when they see the picture. I also showed them a picture of poverty in the third world to evoke a response.*

Music

Another teacher had undertaken 'valuable and helpful' LEA-based training entitled 'Extending Circle Time through Music/Drama', but he had not immediately incorporated it into his sessions 'as it is a "magical time", and I'm not sure if this might be broken if we introduce drama/music and too much moving around.' (year 5/6 teacher, School H)

Others mentioned parallels with learning in music as their activities were sometimes undertaken in a circle. Specifically some noted similarities in terms of 'the same kind of rules and turn taking' and a child standing in the middle of the circle playing a musical instrument.

English and Drama
One teacher had linked the development of thinking and feeling skills in Circle Time with English by asking school leavers to write their memoirs of being in the school (year 5/6 teacher, School E).

In School K, after a boy had had 'time out' of the circle a teacher had used puppets with the children to discuss what they might do when they felt angry.

Some also mentioned using a circle for story time (see also p. 55). The year 3 teacher, School E developed this, by placing the characters in the story at the beginning of Circle Time, by making links with English texts and using Stories for Thinking and Poems for Thinking based on scenarios of bullying, friendship and hate to promote discussion.

Cross-curricular Learning
Some teachers recognised the opportunities Circle Time afforded for dealing with problems generally, or in learning:

> *Sometimes, we might review what we've been doing, or we might discuss what we found difficult. It's quite a good way of getting across any issues they're having. But very broadly, no specific aspects of the curriculum really.*
>
> (Year 2/3 teacher, School B)

> *Circle Time is an opportunity to discuss aspects of curriculum work. With the younger children Circle Time is used to enable them to share news with each other, for the older children it gives them the opportunity to debate.*
>
> (Headteacher, School E)

> *... We've done a few issues, debates about things that we've talked about. I did it at a previous school, we talked about keeping animals at zoos, and some children were for and some were against and we had a sort of round the circle debate. They had to take on a role, some of them were the animals and some of them were the zoo keepers.*
>
> (Year 2/3 teacher, School B)

Depending on the extent to which recognised principles were followed, these experiences might be more about simply learning in a circle rather than deliberately using Circle Time as a specific strategy. Since Circle Time sometimes took place on a carpeted area of the classroom children sometimes confused it with other activities for which they gathered together on the carpet.

3.2.2 Processes and practices within Circle Time

This section considers several approaches to delivering Circle Time: structured, activity based, spontaneous, problem-centred, dealing with emotions, and using games.

A structured approach

A fairly typical approach to Circle Time by a class teacher with a year 2/3 class (22 pupils equally mixed) for 30 minutes at the end of the summer term was as follows:

School ends, holidays begin

The children sat on the carpeted area of the classroom floor, but not in a perfect circle so some could not see each other. The teacher briefly outlined the rule about when to talk, although they did not pass anything around, they simply went around the circle taking turns.

1. She started by asking them 'What did you like most about this year?'

   The children used the starter phrase 'My best bit was ... .'

   They talked very quietly and the teacher encouraged them to make whole sentences.

2. The teacher asked 'What are you looking forward to in the summer holidays?'

   Most talked about an anticipated holiday away. Few pupils passed, though several took a long time to respond.

3. The teacher then asked each pupil to ask another a question: 'Ask each other about your holidays. For example, Where exactly are you going? What are you going to do there?'

For this the children needed to listen to what others had previously said and practice speaking skills. They seemed to find this hard and became a bit fidgety. The teacher told them to cross their legs.

4. The teacher sent one girl to collect the 'magic box', and put it in middle of circle.

   The pupil was asked to find what was inside – 'things you might use on the beach'. The pupil mimed the object and others had to guess what it was.

The pupil choose someone with her/his hand up, and if they answered correctly they went into the middle to mime. During this game all the pupils put up their hands very enthusiastically.

There was a problem in that the pupil miming inevitably had her/his back to half the circle. But this game also moved pupils to different positions in the circle.

5. The teacher gave each child a number. A child then sang 'Who stole the cookie from the cookie jar? No. 3 stole the cookie from the cookie jar.' 'Who, me? Not me. No 7 stole the cookie from the cookie jar.' And so on (see Curry and Bromfield, 1995: 116). Children thoroughly enjoyed this. They went round so all the class had a go.

Near the end three children put up their hands to identify who was left.

Teacher Comments

This class usually did Circle Time once a week in a planned but not always regular slot. The teacher had had training about six years previously with a colleague of Jenny Mosley. She had gradually changed her techniques:

I have modified the methods as I've gone along, yes. I haven't done it this year but I used to do 'Star of the Week'. I did it in one way to start with and that took too long, so I changed it. I didn't start by doing the more interactive bit, the asking questions bit, that's something I've brought in ....

We usually do something around the circle when they have the chance to share something, usually news and to talk. They always get a chance to question because that encourages their listening a bit as well. It might be to explore something that's come up, an issue that's arisen in class about fairness or something, but not often, I think they're a bit too young for that. And then I've got a few different games that we'll use as well, that also involve turn-taking and listening.

We always go through the rules, what it means to be in the circle, listening to each other and valuing what each other says. I always establish that at the beginning. I've made it clear that if they don't want to say anything they only have to say 'pass', and move on. And that nothing negative is said about another child, it's never to be a negative thing that they ask or say an unkind word.

An activity approach

Another favourite Circle Time activity was Child of the Day, sometimes also referred to by teachers as Special Person of the Day (see also p. 90). This was both the shortest Circle Time activity, usually 10–15 minutes in length, and the most frequently observed.

Child of the Day

Child of the Day was chosen as part of the Circle Time activities at the end of a day in which there had been some 'nastiness and tale telling' in the class. A girl was chosen as Child of the Day to sit in the middle of the circle in a group of 24 year 2 children (13 girls and 11 boys) in School D. Children commented positively on her features, qualities and talents (e.g. eyes, hair, shoes, writing). The child who was chosen seemed to thoroughly enjoy what was being said. The teacher commended the comments and said she would type them up and put them on a poster for display in the class. Two girls interviewed later said 'It's fun. We play games. We put people in the middle a lot. I like it when I'm in the middle.' The game seemed to involve, focus and temporarily settle the children.

Most children seemed to be very keen on this activity, which emphasised positive comments and put a child in the spotlight. Even the Child of the Day who started by looking uncomfortable or nervous was 'smiling at the end'.

> In School K a year3 girl told us that 'I'm looking forward to when I'm going to be Child of the Day and deciding what I would say to the questions.' Later she claimed that Circle Time helped to 'understand people better.' Not surprisingly, she could not say how this was brought about, but she said it was because 'You learn a bit more about them. That is the only reason Child of the Day is good.'

However, two other year 4 girls in another class had a more cynical perspective.

Researcher	In Child of the Day everybody has to say positive things; do you think anybody would ever make something up that they didn't really think?
Girl One	No.
Girl Two	Actually, once my friend did when it was T's turn.
Girl One	Cos she didn't like him?
Girl Two	Yes, she didn't like him much, she isn't really that bad tempered, so she didn't want to show her temper so she just made something up.
Researcher	So she didn't pass, she made something up instead?
Girl Two	Yes.

Researcher	What happened then? You knew she had made it up and it wasn't true?
Girl Two	I laughed, but the teacher was thinking what was I laughing at.

It therefore was perhaps not surprising that the most important advice these girls would give to a new girl coming to school was 'Don't tell your secrets'.

Several teachers reported that children had been involved in making up their own rules in Circle Time sessions. These could be class rules but often they were playground rules, in response to playground incidents which needed to be resolved. There were three main Circle Time approaches to dealing with such incidents: organising a spontaneous Circle Time session, planning it into the usual Circle Time session, or as a more informal approach, 'Bubble Time' with specific pupils instead of, or in addition to the main Circle Time (see p. 122)

A spontaneous approach
This example was related by two year 4 girls, School K:

Girl One	We did once when Miss M was here. If we were naughty she would call a Circle Time straight away to sort it out.
Girl Two	She would listen to you, and she would get the person in that class to come over and say sorry.
Researcher	What did you think about that?
Girl One	I think that was a good idea.
Researcher	How did it help you?
Girl One	It made me feel like that I didn't get away with it but at least I had sorted it out more, now.
Girl Two	So it was brought out in the open.
Girl One	Everybody knows.
Researcher	Had something happened to you in particular – would you be willing to talk about it?
Girl One	There was this boy and it was last term when we were year 3's. This boy was picking on me and my best friend. …

And he always used to come up and he always used to call us like racist names and stuff like that. But I told Miss M. ...and Miss M called the class Circle Time and she asked one of the other people that were involved to go and get H to tell [another teacher] what happened and everything and so [he] would like say come and take H and have the Circle Time. So normally Miss M would sort it out in the Circle Time instead of having it go on at play time ... and it made me feel like I am not the only one getting told off, cos I'm not the only one being naughty.

Researcher   So what actually happened in the circle when the boy came from the other class?

Girl One   The people who saw it said things and Miss M would like say write them down and whatever and she'd sort it out and then he'd go back to his class and someone would talk to him about what happened and then he'd try and talk it out with that person whatever.

A problem-centred approach

In the following example, Circle Time is centred to dealing with the problem of being picked on.

Being picked on

The class context

School E, a year 3 group of 28 pupils (11 girls and 17 boys) which included 14 with special needs at some stage and a teaching assistant for 30 minutes. The pupils were perhaps a bit subdued but orderly as the teacher, who had had some training, started them on preparations for Circle Time in a very organised way with clear instructions. In interview she claimed that 'Setting up the Circle Time is very important so that the pupils understand the types of things I am trying to get them to do.' The children who were table monitors cleared the desks and made space for all to sit on or around the carpet – but this was cramped and some, including an autistic child and the teaching assistant, were squashed out at one end. The teacher referred to/reminded the pupils of the rules and explained as they were going along. A pottery flower – referred to by pupils as 'power flower' was circulated. The teacher monitored quality as the rounds progressed and stopped the group and changed activity when appropriate. The pupils seemed supportive, listened, and by the fifth round all had contributed. Most seemed interested and involved.

Circle Time

1. Teacher started: 'Something happened yesterday and a few know why. It was embarrassing. I want you to tell about a time when you were embarrassed. I'll start.'

   'I was embarrassed when...'

   Teacher: 'I dropped my dinner and the whole school looked.'

   Pupil responses:

   'When I gave someone too much money.'

   'When I was walking with my friend back home and tripped over a piece of wire.'

   Teaching Assistant: 'When I sat down and someone had moved the chair and I sat on the floor.'

   'When my mum catched me in the road on my skateboard.'

   Boy: 'When I walked into a lamppost' (laughter).

   'When I fell over on my bike and everyone laughed at me.'

Five girls passed in this round. The teacher commended those who participated.

2. Teacher started a second round: 'I felt very different when ...'

   Teacher: 'When I turned up to the disco in a dress and my friends were wearing trendy trousers.'

   Pupils: 'When I was on my skates without falling over on a ramp.'

   'When I came to this school.'

Pupils found this more difficult so teacher stopped it and explained. Then it continued.

3. Teacher: 'People get picked on because they are different, say because they're wearing a different T shirt, or like in the story we were reading. Can you think of a time when you've been picked on ... ?'

   Started again where the circle had left off.

   Boy: 'Because of my accent.'

   'For years I don't grow I was the smallest.'

   'My friend because I didn't have such good trousers.' (2 other boys agreed)

   Girl: 'Freckle face because I'm the only one in my family with freckles.'

   'Because I was too good for them.'

   'My brother when I didn't want to play.' (One girl who hadn't spoken before said she agreed.)

4. Teacher remarked that if you see someone with glasses or new socks then you shouldn't comment, because it might hurt their feelings. 'What

do you do if you see someone picking on somebody? What can you do? Hands up.'

Nine hands. Question and Answer session, not going round circle.

Pupils: 'Reassure the one being picked on.' 'Ignore them.' 'Ask them to play.' 'Say how would they like it if a person picked on and did it to them.' 'Give them a compliment.'

Teacher endorsed some of these.

5. Teacher commended the class as being generally very good at playing together. 'I want you to think of something the pupil next to you has done really well this year and to tell us about it.'

   Pupil responses included: got better at maths; doing work faster; better writing, handwriting, reading.

6. Teacher: 'Roll the ball to someone and say something about the person you really like.'

   Girl sent it to V 'because she gives lovely smiles'. All the class smiled at this. V was shy and didn't speak. Teacher suggested various reasons why V might be shy. Some thought 'cos she listens.'

   Girl sent ball to teaching assistant 'Because she helps me'.

   Ball to A 'Because he's always ready to help if someone's in trouble.'

   To a girl 'Because she's always sensible and kind.'

   All those mentioned seemed surprised and genuinely pleased. (But what if you never get noticed?)

The teacher stopped the game. 'All those who've not been mentioned put their hands on their shoulders and others put your hands up to say something personal about them.' One said about the girl (with medical condition?) who was on a seat 'Because she never complains.' 'Z because he is very polite when I taught you how to play football.' Z smiled. So did some other boys. Session finished and class went off to assembly.

Pupil reflections
Interview with one girl and two boys, one with special needs.

Researcher	What do you think Circle Time helps you with most?
Girl	To think about how other people feel.
Researcher	And what would you say?
Boy One	Sort out problems.
Researcher	And what would you say?
Boy Two	Don't get yourself into trouble.

Researcher	Can you tell me when you realised that you could see how somebody else felt?
Boy One	Yes, because people normally pick on Z because he's not very good at football. So I asked if I could go on his team sometimes and score some goals for him.
Researcher	And did anything to do with being in Circle Time make you think to ask him to be part of your football?
Boy One	Yeah, because people don't like him really, so whoever is the ref. goes up to him and gives him a red card. So I don't play either and go and play with him instead.
Researcher	Did you become more aware that people didn't like him when you did Circle Time? Or did you know that before?
Boy One	People are making friends with him now because my friends are making friends with him now. Because I'm his friend, they're being bored.
Researcher	And you're good at football are you?
Boy One	Yeah.

Dealing with emotions

One teacher had carefully thought out a planned approach to dealing with the feeling of anger.

Anger

Class context

Year 5/6 pupils (28, 11 girls 17 boys) had arranged chairs in a circle. Teacher asked them to rearrange to form a perfect circle. He had prepared for the session with notes, to which he referred as went along, also occasionally made notes of his own. From time to time teacher explained rules, did some orchestrating, was a little directive, also asked questions and gave examples. Teacher did some intervention, exploration, information giving, and, after each round, some diagnosis and evaluation.

Pupils were attentive and very keen to participate, seemed to enjoy it, also fairly competitive. Overall there was a sense of a group, but of cliques within. Pupils were helpful to one another. Although this was actually one of the more self-disciplined classes observed, there was one incident when two boys giggled and did not exercise enough self-control to stop. The teacher asked another pupil to put down the conch so he could talk and then asked them to turn their chairs around to face out of the circle for the rest of the round. Then they were asked if they could behave and allowed to rejoin the circle. One of the boys started laughing again, but managed to overcome it.

Circle Time

1. A welcoming round. The teacher introduced this with 'Hello ... . Welcome to Circle Time.' Each child asked to speak to next child on the right. All did this round the circle. (Strangely, although he was friendly, he did not introduce the researchers to the pupils.)

2. Teacher explained the next active game. He asked them to sit in order of the letter of their mother's first name, without talking. All children then got up and made letters with their hands. The teacher reminded them to help each other. Cooperative negotiating by mouthing and sign language. This was amusing and the children appeared to enjoy it and take it quite seriously. The children shuffled round to let others in. The teacher debriefed and commented. Some clearly managed much better than others because of their social skills, initiative and inventiveness. It was particularly difficult for those with letters in the middle of the alphabet. In the end the group had done quite well, with only a couple in the wrong place.

3. The teacher asked the pupils to 'Change places across the circle if you've ever seen anything on TV which made you angry.'

   Next round: 'If you've ever made your Mum or Dad angry.'

   Then: 'If your Mum or Dad made you angry this week.'

   Next: 'If you've ever done something because you were angry and you had to do something about it.'

   Teacher: 'Today we were talking about being angry. I get angry when I see on TV that some children are not treated well by their parents.' Explained what meant by 'angry'.

   Asked pupils to go round the circle saying: 'I get angry when ...'

Examples: 'My mum yells at me.' 'I see animals being killed on TV.' (Several like this.) 'When my sister beat me up.' (Laughter at the latter: subsequently learnt it was because the boy's sister, a twin, was also in the circle.) 'When my brother is horrible to me.'

Teacher reminded them of the importance of listening to others and reprimanded two boys who continued to giggle and made them turn their chairs to look outside the circle.

Girl and boy: 'When I get blamed for what I haven't done.' Animals not getting fed.' 'When I have to clean my room.' 'Hearing children have been abused or killed.'

The two boys were allowed to turn their chairs around.

Teacher asked them to think what happens to their body and mind when they get angry. Put out your hand anyone who wants to say what happens.

Examples: 'Throw something around.' 'Get dizzy.' 'My mind gets blocked and ...' 'All the happiness inside me shoots out.' 'I lose control, I think what am I going to do, I want to destroy everything in sight.'

Teacher asked what causes anger? What made the cave man angry? Suggestions: could have had something stolen from him, attacked or physically harmed.

'What is the body getting ready to do?' Explained fight or flight.

Asked: 'Is it a good idea for you to go and punch someone?' All: 'No!'

'What do you do if you're really angry?'

'What strategies do you have if you are angry?'

Examples: 'Try and calm down and think about something else.'

'Go and do something, like acrobatics.' 'Write it all down on a piece of paper and then tear it up.' Teacher commended this idea. 'Talk to someone about it.' 'Talk to other people about it and forget it.'

Teacher made some statements. 'If you agree say so.' (As a group.) (Most did):

'I sometimes get angry – hot inside and I have to let the anger out.'

'People I know sometimes make me angry.'

'I feel I have to hurt myself.' (Some said yes to this.)

'I feel I need to attack something.'

Teacher summarised. 'So we have strong feelings about anger. And sometimes we need to do something about it.' Reminded them of the constructive suggestions made about how to deal with anger.

Told them five minutes left.

4. Played game where as a group they were supposed to count out loud to ten with only one person saying a number. They had several attempts at this and although some children held up fingers to show what they wanted to say the group didn't get past the number five. They were actually too keen and did not allow others enough leeway, hence their lack of success with the task. (Perhaps this was affected by the teacher saying another group had done it in a quicker time?)

5. Finally the children were asked to say goodbye to one another, then to bow their head. The teacher was to be chosen last.

Using games

Teachers who followed a more structured approach or felt more confident about practising Circle Time were more likely to include games as well as discussion, passing an object or special child of the day strategies. Games could help to change mood and pace and mostly made for a lot of fun and noise. Some games were complex and teachers found that they had to be modified to take account of group size, gender mix and pupils' boisterousness. Sometimes children did not realise they were learning from games. For example, a teacher who had done parachute games with two classes, borrowing a real parachute from the RAF, noted that children did not realise until towards the end of the game that they were working together, they just thought they were having fun. Teachers had to develop skills to deal with transitions from games to the more serious exercises in structured Circle Time.

The Parachute Game was in fairly common use, and appeared to make an impression, give pupils enjoyment and develop a sense of belonging to the group. Although it required quite a lot of direction and organisation by the teacher, it did not require any talking from the pupils.

The parachute game

In School K 35 year 3/4 pupils in their PE kit were sitting in the hall in a circle. Their class teacher and two other adult helpers paid a lot of attention to making sure the circle was as perfect as possible.

While sitting down they did stretching exercises. They seemed to enjoy these, perhaps especially as the hall was quite cold. They were quiet and paid attention, following instructions well. The teacher then sent two pupils to get the parachute, and then lay it out in the middle of the circle. Every child in the circle then had to hold the edge of it.

The teacher went round the circle numbering the children from 1–6, repeatedly. Then they all stood up, holding the parachute, and moved it up and down. The teacher called out a number between 1–6 and all those with that number had to run under the parachute and swap places. They enjoyed this fun and ran around frantically, colliding.

The second game was to choose someone who was to try and catch the 'fruit', actually a few coloured balls, while the children sitting down waved the parachute. The teacher encouraged the children to 'work together to move the parachute'.

A small disruption led the teacher to ask 'What do you do if I blow the whistle?', all replied 'Stop'.

Thirdly, they played a game called 'Cat and Mouse'. The mouse was to go under the parachute, the cat then went on top and tried to 'catch' the mouse by patting his shoulder. During this the other children waved the parachute.

At the end all the children clapped each other.

3.3 Key findings and issues

♦ Teachers' aims for using Circle Time varied according to the school, class, pupil ages and particular circumstances. In interviews, they chose three main aims: fostering self-esteem, encouraging pupils to respect themselves and others and developing communication skills.

♦ Circle Time was delivered in diverse ways: integrated into the curriculum and teaching approach, timetabled and mixed ability, through PSE, in small group work, involving other adults and making curriculum links to Circle Time.

♦ Within Circle Time, teachers used several main approaches: structured, activity based, spontaneous, a problem-centred and a planned approach to dealing with emotions, as well as using games in Circle Time.

4 Issues in Circle Time in practice

Observation of Circle Time was one of the key aspects of the research. The main focus of interest was to observe, record, interpret and discuss with teachers and pupils their experiences of Circle Time. Circle Time was thus regarded as a continuous event or as a set of activities and in terms of certain features and processes of the strategy, such as practical matters, interactions, behaviour and so on in the class environment (see Appendix 1). The research also explored the extent to which Circle Time reinforced or contrasted with other class experiences in terms of pedagogic strategies, teacher-pupil and pupil-pupil relationships.

4.1 Practical issues

Practical matters (layout and the formation of the circle, sitting and seating, the place of the teacher, passing an object and the duration and timing) were critical to the success of Circle Time.

4.1.1 Layout

The layout of the primary class space often required considerable alteration to enable participants to sit in a circle. Sometimes, a lack of space meant that classes had to move, for example, to the music room, TV room or hall, or – during summer months – outside on the grass. These moves might require timetabling for dedicated use.

> You need a lot of space. Even the hall is not a particularly friendly space, especially if talking confidentially.

One class settled on the stage of the school hall and drew the curtains. The children appeared to enjoy the sense of privacy this gave them (year 6, School N).

Privacy was an issue, especially if the class was meeting in a public space. One teacher had put a notice on the door requesting not to be interrupted and another concurred:

> I think the difficulty is sometimes trying to get privacy because you can

be in quite an intimate conversation with the children and someone will come in with a message or a phone call.

(Special needs teacher, School B)

In many classes, some rearrangement of the furniture was required to create enough space for all to sit in a circle. Whilst this might be undertaken with smooth efficiency, it sometimes provided opportunities for disruption and friction just prior to the Circle Time activity itself. In School F, the year 2 pupils reported that they did not always move to sit in a circle, as this necessitated the moving of furniture.

However, handbooks and manuals emphasise (and children are often aware of) the importance of enabling all pupils to be able to see each other, make eye contact and participate. The headteacher of School E commented: 'they're so egocentric at this age and why should the teacher always be the focal point?' Other shapes, such as an oblong or a rectangle, obscure sight lines and can be exclusive, especially where conditions are cramped and acoustics poor.

Many sessions were observed where a circle was not formed (possibly because of class size), to the pupils' dissatisfaction. It could lead to disruptive behaviour (for example, in School D, year 5/6) if the children were constantly leaning forward on their chairs to try to see one another (see below).

4.1.2 Sitting and seating

There was variation in classes as to whether they sat on chairs or on the (carpeted) floor. Older pupils were more likely to sit on chairs and it was more difficult for older teachers to sit on the floor. In some classes chairs were allowed when there were visitors present or if there was likely to be more movement in the group during the playing of games. Children often expressed a preference for sitting on chairs 'because chairs are more comfortable'.

Carpet versus chairs

The year 5/6 class in School H was in an 1870s building in rather cramped conditions, with windows and a gallery above for quiet work. During the year the class had changed its Circle Time arrangement from sitting on the carpet to sitting on chairs, with the curtains over windows at wall level closed. At the teacher's request the children arranged the circle, with a certain amount of commotion, but efficiently. According to the teacher 'the advantage of the chairs is that they [the pupils] think they are more grown up and it's also easier to change places. But it's more difficult to set up, especially in restricted space.' In the Circle Time session observed the teacher paid particular attention to the circle formation, asking some children to move back to try to ensure a perfect circle so all could see each other. The pupils interviewed were able to compare their sitting experiences of Circle Time and express their views.

Researcher	Explain to me what happens when you do Circle Time. Just tell me what happens from right at the beginning from the time he says 'It's time to do Circle Time now.'
Girl One	We put our chairs in a circle.
Researcher	How long did it take you to get used to doing that?
Girl One	Last year we just used to sit down.
Boy One	On the carpet and we used to have a conch in the middle. Now we've changed it and we have done all sorts of number games.
Girl One	And we did dressing up in masks.
Boy One	And you have got to act out that person.
Researcher	What's the difference between sitting on the carpet and sitting on the chairs as far as you're concerned?
Boy Two	You can't see everyone sitting on the chairs because sometimes people lean forward on the chairs and you can't see.
Researcher	Does that make a difference?
Girl One	Yes, because if say somebody is talking and people are leaning forward you can't see them and you can't hear them properly.
Boy One	You have got to get a perfect circle so that you can see everyone.
Researcher	What's important about seeing everyone?
Girl One	If people like think 'Oh they're all looking at me' and if you're like sitting back and listening then I can say whatever I like …
Researcher	So you want everybody to sit back and listen really?
Girl One	Yes
Researcher	Do you all feel the same?
All	Yes
Researcher	Do you think it's better on the chairs than the carpet?
Boy One	On the chairs it's nicer, you can sit in your normal position.

Girl One	And on the chairs you can play good games. ... Because you have all the chairs in a circle and you don't have to change places. And if you are sitting in a circle everybody would get up and you would lose the circle.
Researcher	So, but you still prefer on the carpet?
Boy Two	Yes.
Researcher	Can you say why?
Boy Two	Because you feel more like a group.
Boy One	If you have a rectangle or something ... a circle is a kind of grouply shape it's not like two sides ...
Girl Two	And if it's a circle like it doesn't stop at one point it keeps going.

4.1.3 Teacher in the circle

Another important practical issue, stressed in Circle Time manuals, is the inclusion of the teacher in the circle and most significantly at the same level (on chairs or on the floor) as the pupils. As one school-based trainer emphasised, 'it changes mood instantly'. However, in some cases, children were observed on the floor and the teacher in a chair. Is the idea of the teacher sitting at the same level as the children of subtle significance for the Circle Time ethos, suggesting she/he is no longer an authority on what happens in the exchanges, just another human being? Or is this levelling of status merely token equality? Is not the teacher still in authority in charge of orchestrating the Circle Time?

4.1.4 Passing an object

Circle Time manuals recommend the passing round of an object during Circle Time. Yet quite often we observed no object was circulated and pupils raised their hands to signal that they wished to speak. In a few cases the children just took turns. One teacher commented, 'I've done it when they've passed around a special toy, something to get hold of, but these children are quite confident, they don't need a prop.' Occasionally a teacher forgot to bring an object.

In some groups the object passed around remained the same, a (magic) stone, a pinecone, a book, a starfish, a conch, a paperweight, a soft toy. One year 5/6 class always passed a conch. The teacher felt it had various analogies. 'It is delicate but also represents Circle Time for them. There is something special about it. The ideas go into the conch. Their thoughts and ideas are carried around in it, locked up.' But in many classes the object could be one chosen or provided by the children, or a random item which could be passed easily (e.g. a battery). Sometimes pupils were observed wanting to exchange the object in order to allow that person to have a turn, rather than passing it around the circle; sometimes, usually in a game, this was allowed. Occasionally a teacher would vary the technique and not go around the circle.

4.1.5 Timing and time during the school day

The timing of Circle Time depended on whether it was timetabled or used as a spontaneous learning strategy. Timetabled Circle Time frequently took place at the end of the day, and on Friday. Whereas a teacher might feel 'It's just a nice way to round off Friday afternoon' pupils might not focus on calm reflection, listening and speaking, but more on the end of the school day, leaving school and going home. There was some incidental evidence that schools were beginning to evaluate the most effective time for Circle Time.

Some teachers were more inclined to use Circle Time spontaneously, especially if there was a behaviour problem in the playground or classroom. On occasion children had requested a Circle Time session in response to an incident and the teacher might negotiate with them to defer it to the end of the school day.

The time devoted to Circle Time varied greatly from school to school and class to class, depending on whether it was timetabled, but teachers might reduce the time if hard pressed. An interviewee made the following observation:

> *I think what we do is sufficient, bearing in mind that the demands on our time are getting greater and greater, the free time is gradually reducing. The literacy hour takes up one session a day, the numeracy hour another, so we're left with a third session to do everything else in.*
> (Year 2 teacher, School A)

The Circle Time sessions observed varied from ten to 45 minutes, with older children usually receiving longer sessions.

4.2 The teacher's role

Even where teachers are physically at the same level in the circle, they nevertheless remain in charge of the children and the educational experience offered. Whilst Circle Time may appear simple, it requires careful management and orchestration of the children and the processes to achieve inclusion and equality of opportunity, differentiation and progression. Teachers have to be in control of the overall purpose, plan and structure, whilst leaving space for flexible and free-flowing contributions and activities. They have to facilitate the beginning, the building of phases, pace and closure as well as securing appropriate behaviour and respect for rules

Children generally recognised the teacher's continuing authority: 'He speaks as part of a group he's not better than anyone else'; 'He speaks more than us because he has to tell us what to do'; 'Because it's like the games and stuff he has to start and things…'.

4.2.1 Getting started

Good practice requires teachers to pay attention to the transition from the preceding activity to the Circle Time experience, by giving clear instructions about moving into a circle and explicit indications about expected behaviour. One year 2 teacher in School M ensured children were settled before she began by reminding them, 'Put your hands in your laps. Circle Time is a good time for speaking and listening.' She also gave an example of what children might say as an appropriate response before starting each activity. However, the teachers we observed seldom explained to the pupils the sequence or objectives of Circle Time rounds and activities in advance. This seemed to be an accepted aspect of its mystique which enabled the teacher to retain control of the learning strategy, to implement a prepared plan or to respond flexibly to the pace and contributions of the pupils. However, some older pupils could articulate a sense of the rhythm, structure and purpose of some Circle Time experiences.

Building up a sense of confidence in, and belonging to, the group was fundamental to Circle Time activities. However, as getting started might be difficult, teachers sometimes used an icebreaker activity, such as 'patting knees, clapping hands and clicking fingers', or a game like 'Silent

Statements' (anyone who plays a musical instrument has to swap seats silently with someone else who plays a musical instrument) or 'Chair on the Right' (used for example, to help 'to avoid sexist splits in the peer group').

4.2.2 Building structure

In order to be a structured learning activity Circle Time has to follow certain rules. One trained teacher who used Circle Time, both as part of PSE and spontaneously for behavioural reasons, claimed that the most useful thing she had learned was 'insisting on the rules'. Teachers frequently had to remind children of the rules and whilst they often began the Circle Time session (particularly with younger children) by talking through the rules, both the rules cited and the emphases varied.

Some teachers stressed the procedural rule that the children could only talk when holding the object passed around, but some children were too eager to speak and did not remember. Teachers dealt with serious breaches of the rules by threatening to remove persistent offenders from the group or asking children to turn their chairs to face outwards, or to remove themselves from the circle until their self-command suggested that they could be invited to return and participate.

Other teachers placed more emphasis on the social and moral aspects of the procedures, such as not saying anything hurtful, not discussing what is said in Circle Time afterwards, or with anyone outside the group.

4.2.3 Keeping contributions going

How does the teacher keep the dialogue flowing around the circle? On what kinds of pupil contributions does the teacher comment? When does the teacher give praise or reproof? How can pupils be discouraged from offering superficial contributions and how can they be encouraged to think carefully and build on what has been said before? Pace was a significant issue in many Circle Time activities and was frequently related to 'passing' (whether or not a child chose to speak), which could require other pupils to wait patiently for what appeared to be a lengthy time. Another factor was the extent to which some children merely repeated what another child had said. Some teachers exhorted children 'only [to] speak if you've thought of something different'. When children got restless with waiting some teachers asked children to stand up and turn around, or take part in a game in the circle. Some teachers gave feedback, encouragement and praise for responses; others valued all Circle Time contributions irrespective of relevance or salience.

4.2.4 'Passing'

Teachers needed to be aware of, and deal consistently with, pupils who 'passed' when their turn came to speak. Some teachers who remembered, returned to those who had 'passed' at the end of the round; others asked who had 'passed', which enabled some confident pupils to claim a second opportunity to speak.

Teachers also need to explain their reasons for differential treatment. Some teachers encouraged participation as they went around the circle; saying, for example, 'She's just thinking', or 'Brilliant! He's said something this week'. But others seemed to think that if a child wished to 'pass', the desire for privacy should be respected. However, teachers found that, as the group spent more time doing Circle Time, fewer pupils 'passed' and when they did, it was to take 'thinking time' before they responded.

4.2.5 Behaviour

Some younger children and those with behavioural difficulties had problems remaining quiet and sensible during a Circle Time round, especially in large groups (some had over 30 children). Games could increase the amount of boisterous activity and there was usually a certain amount of fidgeting, scraping of feet, whispering and so on, which could be off putting. Sometimes peers exerted a certain amount of pressure on others to conform, for example by 'shushing' a child who attempted to interrupt another. Teachers varied immensely in how they dealt with disruptions. 'Time out' procedures were usually temporary so that the child(ren) could still hear the circle activities and later be easily reabsorbed in the group. Where there was a whole-school approach, children could be sent to another class and teacher to provide mutual support for teachers.

4.3 Participation and non-participation

Whilst some children relished a chance to speak and took every opportunity to do so, others had to find their voice, and some were markedly reluctant to speak out. Teachers noted which children participated and who did not. A few teachers seemed to think that the rule of speaking only when holding the object gave quiet and shy children an equal chance to participate. Others intimated that the very shape of the circle could facilitate contributions. However, they did not seem to have given much thought as to how they could improve children's participation and they may have underestimated the potential effect of inhibiting factors (see Chapter 6).

> One young teacher, who had been doing Circle Time for three or four years, had had training, and took preparation seriously, acknowledged 'I have not had any reservations with the children I've used it with. I'm not sure how I would deal with a child who could not get used to Circle Time.' (year 5/6 teacher, School H)

> Another reflected: 'I might eventually get around to passing round a microphone or something special and see if that will encourage them.' (year 1 teacher, School A).

4.3.1 Group size

The number of pupils in a class affects the degree of participation:

> *I had 22 and that takes long enough really to get round the circle. And next year I'll have 34, which will be difficult I think. You're talking about twice as many children, twice as long for them to sit and listen. They all get the chance to do things at the moment, whereas with more children that will get more difficult, I think, with younger children as it means them sitting and listening longer. You don't want it really small because then you don't get the balanced ideas and opinions coming out, but I think over 30 it could start getting a bit tricky.*
>
> (Year 2/3 teacher, School B)

By breaking up into three groups of 14, the School G nursery had improved management and participation in Circle Time and teachers felt the children's confidence and self-esteem had been enhanced.

4.3.2 Pupil characteristics

Pupils' personalities, gender and cultural conditioning (see p. 100) can be important factors as to whether or not they contribute in the circle.

> The headteacher and some staff in one infant school with pupils mainly from Asian backgrounds did not favour Circle Time, although it was practised by the nursery teachers. The headteacher thought it was 'quite threatening for children outside the family circle because it puts the child in the centre of attention and doesn't offer a way of drawing the child out.' He considered that many children are rather insecure and should not be put 'on the spot' while others are waiting for them to speak. He thought that 'some children are garrulous, whilst others become elected mutes' and that gender and kinship exerted an implicit influence, especially as there were more boys than girls in school. He thought Circle Time should be a 'therapeutic activity' used occasionally.
>
> (School N)

4.3.3 Peer pressure

Another possible factor might be peer pressure.

> *You ask for an opinion and they've said it just because their friend did, rather than honestly think about the question. ... I've never experienced anyone not joining in because of the peer pressure ... but I think peer encouragement sometimes will make them join in. Like if they get the friendly smiles or nudges from their friends.*
>
> (Year 2/3 teacher, School B)

4.4 Sensitivity, confidentiality and disclosure

Many teachers had experienced times when sensitive issues were discussed, confidences shared or confidentiality broken outside the group and disclosures made. Such episodes raised ethical concerns, called professional judgement to account and sometimes there was a need to invoke established procedures and practices in response.

4.4.1 Sensitivity

Teachers needed to be well informed about the children's characteristics and circumstances to minimise incidents which might give rise to hurt feelings or negative learning experiences. Primary class teachers, who spend much time with and get to know the backgrounds and sensitivities of individual pupils have an advantage over a PSE coordinator. Circle Time topics often intentionally reached into or explored sensitive or potentially revealing areas of experience. For example, after a half-term break one reception teacher asked children to 'Close your eyes and think of something which makes your home really special'. The diversity of responses was quite revealing of different life circumstances (School J). Another who had used Circle Time to prepare the class for the up coming summer holidays reflected:

I think sometimes it can reinforce things for those children that don't have so much because they become aware that others have exciting things to look forward to. ... They could have been listening to all the things that the others are doing, all the exciting holidays that they're going on and they're not. I'm aware of that and trying to build those children up afterwards if I feel that there could have been negative feeling about it.

(Year 2/3 teacher, School B)

The same teacher, knowing pupils' backgrounds, was also aware of other potential pitfalls:

If it's Mother's Day you might talk about mums but if you knew that there were children in the circle who didn't have a mum around then obviously you wouldn't do that with that class. So you have to be quite selective and careful.

(Year 2/3 teacher, School B)

Another teacher, who had not had Circle Time training, had learnt to be more sensitive through an ill-judged experience

One session I asked everyone to chose a friend and at the end one child had not got chosen and got very upset. It was a mistake on my part, so you need to be careful. I had to talk individually to the child, the parents and the group.

(Teacher, School B)

A year 5/6 teacher in School H had encountered a sensitive issue when she allowed children to suggest their own topics for Circle Time. An adopted child had asked to give a presentation on adoption. He prepared the presentation himself and the other children were attentive, asked questions and shared their views.

In response to 'Are there any pupils who regularly don't participate?' one teacher unexpectedly gave another insight into sensitivity:

If it's done within the classroom all the children take part, the only reason a child would be withdrawn would be if you are talking about that child and it was felt it would be sensitive for them to be there.

This appears to relate closely to issues of disclosure and the need for confidentiality. Some pupils were clearly concerned about their privacy, whereas others were not necessarily aware of how their actions made others feel. Circle Time manuals emphasise that children should not mention other pupils by name, but when year 4 children in School L were asked to talk about 'One thing that you've failed on this year – that's been a real problem – that we can work on as a class' some children mentioned both teachers' and other pupils' names (e.g. 'I don't like X picking on me.'; 'Getting used to Mrs B's class and hard work'; 'J doesn't let me play football.' The teacher subsequently said she was 'bothered' if children used other pupils' names negatively.

Although some Circle Time manuals advocate Bubble Time – one-to-one talks with individual pupils about specific problems – few teachers seemed to use this technique to follow up sensitive issues or disclosures. An experienced Circle Time teacher reported:

If there are sensitive times I let the children say what they want, I don't stop them mid-sentence. I move them quickly on, see them afterwards and follow it up. I make mental notes. If I have concerns I talk about it with colleagues.

(Year 3 teacher, School J)

Thus, as part of the preparation for and implementation of Circle Time, teachers needed to be able to follow through with pastoral approaches, where appropriate, and to be assured of the support of colleagues in implementing recognised procedures and practices.

4.4.2 Confidentiality

Several teachers mentioned the importance of group dynamics to develop and respect the confidentiality in the group.

The acting headteacher of School N reported that, both pre- and post-training, teachers had expressed concerns about their ability to deal with children's disclosures and expressions of feeling in Circle Time. It was 'potentially a can of worms'. They were dealing with children's fears. He wondered if teachers could cope with developing relationships and respond appropriately. Staff were generally positive about Circle Time and the senior management wanted to involve all staff, to help with school ethos, behaviour and discipline, but they 'wanted teachers to be aware of the pros and cons'. The teacher of the class observed in Circle Time was concerned about 'possible confidences compromised'.

In the nursery environment of School G, the teachers were concerned about sensitive issues and the privacy of young children. They followed social services guidelines and did not ask leading questions, but were guided by what a child wanted to tell. However, sometimes children made up stories. One girl claimed that her baby brother had died, but when the teacher checked this out with an aunt and another teacher she discovered it was untrue.

A Special Needs Coordinator in School B who used Circle Time with a group who had problems with friendships explained: 'That kind of talk helped them to empathise with each other. I was surprised that they kept to confidentiality, especially as they were difficult children. Circle Time seems to bring on a more mature approach. I've never seen it not work, but I don't know how it works. We have talked about some tricky areas.'

4.4.3 Disclosure

Some teachers recognised that Circle Time experiences could bring into the open delicate boundaries between the public and private, of what was appropriate and inappropriate, in a class environment and of what was normal for an individual pupil. Such issues required their discretion and professional judgement. There is likely to be professional diversity as to what is acceptable and what is not but clear rules are required as to when immediate intervention and/or further action are required.

A year 5/6 teacher in School H said that, if he felt a child was saying something totally inappropriate, he would ask the child to put the conch on the floor in front of him or her and then he would get up and touch the conch and speak. But this would be rare.

Many teachers claimed they would follow up on disclosures, for example:

If something came up, it hasn't happened that much, I must admit, but I would do if I was concerned with their response. There's been something I've been concerned about – that A tells me that he always spends his holidays in McDonalds. So I talked to him about that and I delved further, because his mum works in McDonalds. I would follow that kind of thing up.

(Year 2/3 teacher, School B)

Often I'll say, 'Can we talk about that more after the Circle Time?' and obviously then you have to follow procedure. It has to go further. Sometimes children know that their language will become inappropriate and they have to be reminded of that, because you're creating an informal atmosphere. We were sharing some jokes the other day and one child was saying a joke and he was obviously aware it wasn't suitable ... I think when told ... he became upset then. So sometimes because you've broken the barriers they find it hard that you still have some boundaries. It's hard because you're opening and closing boundaries within Circle Time. Which is why I think we have to have certain criteria which they know they have to follow. You are on dangerous ground or potentially dangerous ground. You may hear something and you know these children so you know if they're saying it for effect.

(Special needs coordinator, School B)

In School E, a child had indicated something about treatment at home which had led to the teacher reporting the disclosure to the headteacher, who had responsibility for child protection. The recognised procedure was followed and in this way, the mother became aware of the behaviour of her partner.

4.5 Critical reflections

From observations and interviews, three factors may be identified as contributing to the quality and success of Circle Time: the ethos of the circle, the topics discussed and teaching and learning styles.

4.5.1 The ethos of the circle

The ethos of the circle is a combination of factors concerning communication, relationships and the learning environment which lead to good Circle Time sessions. Whilst these share features with other effective and pleasurable teaching and learning activities, there are distinctive organisational features of Circle Time which invite comment and further exploration.

Firstly, Circle Time embodies a number of values, some of which are evident in its essential procedures and practices. For example, seating pupils and teacher in a circle and at the same level (on the floor, on chairs) is intended to convey a sense of equality. Is this made explicit to the children? Is it artificial? Does the teacher sit at the same level as the children in any other lesson? Do the pupils see it as significant? What meaning do they give to it? Is the teacher, nevertheless, still in a position of authority? In Circle Time, pupils should listen to the speaker with interest and respect. Are they clearly made aware of the need to do this by their teachers? What skills are involved and how can they be helped to learn to listen? Does it work in practice? Are listening skills and respect or tolerance transferred to other learning environments?

The communicative competence and personality of the teacher can set the tone, especially for teacher-pupil relationships, and the atmosphere of the group. This seems to apply all the more in bringing about an enjoyable and effective experience of Circle Time. Key features include the move into a circle, changed learning activity, pace, verbal involvement of the children and games, although they do not mask the serious points of some discussion and activities for at least some perceptive pupils. As in other teaching and learning experiences, the teacher needs to capitalise on the 'teachable moment' and effect smooth transitions.

> One teacher in School N allowed year 6 pupils to ask a question to stimulate discussion; asking questions was apparently normal class practice. One girl suggested 'What do you want to be when you grow up?' and each pupil responded. Another girl observed that 'Everyone might not get to do what they want.' The teacher went with the spirit of the group and asked: 'What could you do to try to get where you wanted?' Pupils explored various suggestions: 'trying harder', 'having a dream', 'having an aspiration', 'having lots of answers', and, being realistic, 'I know I haven't a good chance of X but I have a chance of Y'. There was an awareness that, locally, there were 'more people than jobs' but that it was important to have hope; one girl reported that her grandmother, over 60, was doing a new job in church.

Establishing trust and cooperation between pupils and with the teacher can promote social and interpersonal learning. In the words of a special needs teacher in School B:

I think you also need a certain rapport with the children ... some teachers may find talking about feelings more difficult and may be uncomfortable with it. You need a good rapport first.

The atmosphere in the group can be highly variable and run through a range of emotional expressions. Primary classes spend much of their time together, but beyond this, a sense of group belonging seems to be an important aspect of Circle Time for pupils. One group, for example, which had had a bad reputation in school, appeared friendly, supportive, curious, keen to ask and answer questions and shared sympathetic laughter in Circle Time.

4.5.2 Appropriate topics

The selection of discussion topics or activities which are suitable for pupils' ages and ability levels and appropriate for Circle Time requires the professional judgement of a teacher who knows the children well. Whilst a researcher or inspector cannot claim such specific knowledge, the following example indicates some differences in perception about a Circle Time experience and difficulties of evaluation.

Sharing fears

Context

In School H a Reception group of 15 (eight girls and seven boys) undertook their second Circle Time session. The teacher aimed to improve language skills to 'give them confidence and the right to express their feelings'. The teacher, sitting on a chair, began by explaining in child friendly way about Circle Time. The children were sitting patiently on the carpet in part of a large open plan area, but could not all see each other. Children chose 'Talking Ted' from a number of soft toys. Teacher checked children's understanding that they should not talk unless they were holding Ted, but she needed to remind them from time to time during the session. She commented on children's responses and asked further questions. There was no sense of a group, although there was no hostility. Pupils appeared quite egocentric, even a little competitive given the topic of discussion. All spoke independently and did not relate to what others said. There was some chatting which subsided. Mostly the children were very attentive when listening to one another. One child wanted to answer all the teacher's questions.

Circle Time

1. Talking Ted. Pupils introduced themselves and passed Ted around, possibly as a way of rehearsing use of Ted.

2. Little Bear. Teacher referred to the story of the little bear, about night time and the dark, which they had read previously. 'What did he feel in bed in the dark? What do you feel? She asked the children to give Ted a cuddle and 'tell us how you feel at night time'.

Most of the children said they were not scared but others expressed some degree of fear:

S had a video which helped her go to sleep. Sometimes she was scared 'because it's really dark'. Calls Mum and Dad. Said 'Don't be frightened'. Makes her feel OK.

G is a bit scared when Mummy is going out, not so scared if Mummy is there.

H likes the dark. With teacher spoke about how the dark makes a difference and how some animals come out.

E 'felt sad' about the dark. Teacher elicited that dreams make her sad. Goes to Mummy. 'She calms me down.'

B gets cross, as he hates going to sleep. 'Cos I'm lonely and I don't have any teddies … I like the rain.'

T scared. Had had a bad dream about spiders. New school changed into a spider's web. He escaped from the pink spider. Less scared when switched the light on.

A 'when I have my stories it makes me feel a bit brave'.

Teacher thanked them for sharing their feelings and telling what they do when they feel frightened in bed in the dark. She stressed that 'it's most important if you feel something, you need to share it. Feelings are just how we are.'

Researcher comments

Though this was charming to observe and was conducted by the teacher in a very kind and non-threatening way, it might have caused some children to feel more fearful or self-conscious about revealing and reliving their fears. It did not really provide any constructive suggestions about how to deal with the fears. On the other hand, it did foster their listening skills and giving of attention, as well as allowing them an opportunity to express their emotions and thoughts in a group. By so doing children were able to learn that some other children share their anxieties and also have to learn how to cope with them.

Teacher comments

The teacher thought Circle Time developed confidence and patience. She also saw it as contributing to baseline assessments for speaking and listening.

Pupil Comments

In interview subsequently two girls and two boys, aged four and five, seemed to have no concerns about the topics under discussion and their expressions of feelings. On the contrary, these children claimed that through Circle Time they learnt to listen (even though one boy experienced this as challenging and boring), to pay attention, to feel better about themselves, to say how they think and feel and to work better in class.

However, several teachers, who were reflective about their practice and who seemed from our observations to be quite successful in running Circle Time, could not identify the topics and specific techniques which work well and contribute to a good Circle Time experience. This seems an odd response when some teachers and schools are investing quite some time in Circle Time activities and have weighty expectations of it.

4.5.3 Modifying pedagogy

Some teachers adapted and developed their own Circle Time techniques, enhancing their expectations of pupils and evolving the rules and norms. The following example, using data triangulation from headteacher, teachers, pupil and researcher, illustrates how one teacher modified practices. It shows that teachers have to bear in mind many complex considerations when adapting strategies such as Circle Time to their own mixed classes. Different practices may emerge within schools. Even an apparently simple activity can raise ethical concerns and demonstrate the values issues in pedagogy. Such an example might be used for teachers to consider in continuing professional development

Special Person of the Day

In School A Circle Time was limited, as a part of PSE, to a short weekly session focusing on Special Person of the Day selected by each class from names (which included the teacher and special needs assistant) in a tin. The person sat in the centre of the circle and children were invited to make positive comments about him/her.

Teacher's Aim

Over the year the year 1 teacher was trying to take a cognitive developmental approach and the children interviewed had clearly grasped the rule which had evolved. The teacher was attempting to make pupils justify what they said and make their responses more meaningful. 'Before now, they've only ever said "He's kind and helpful" or "I like his writing" and I've thought, "Well, they're just saying what other people have said, they're not really thinking about it, so we're going to focus in now, we're going to think about what they mean." I am consciously doing that – thinking through what they've said and whether they realise what it means.'

Pupils' response

Two boys and two girls from this group said they understood there were rules to keep in Circle Time: 'Don't talk when other people are talking, if you say they're kind and helpful, you have to say why they're kind and helpful, if you say they've done a nice picture, you have to say which picture.' 'You can't just say anything.' 'You have to put your brain on, your thinking cap on.' The children all liked the Special Person in Circle Time 'Especially when its you.' Their positive statements were backed up with examples, including inspection of work (e.g. writing or painting) and reinforcement by the teacher.

The children were also clear that 'You've just got to think and speak. ... If somebody doesn't speak, we carry on and we go back to them, and if they don't speak again, we do it again; if they don't speak again, the teacher says "That's not very nice!".' The children interviewed all felt it was always easy to find something nice to say about someone, 'but some people don't think it.' The teacher felt that children were influenced by their peers because, for example, they would copy comments, but even those who had fallen out with each other always found something positive to say: 'nobody's ever even tried to say something negative'. 'They're always told that if it were their Special Day, would they like someone to say something not very nice about them, but I've never actually had to say this in Circle Time.'

Teacher's evaluation

'Its quite effective, they do think hard about what they're saying.' 'I think we'll see how we go, maybe even ask the pupils what they'd like to do.' Each 'Special Person' is given a certificate with the positive remarks to share with their parents, who are informed about the Special Person Days in the school brochure and at introductory parents' evenings. But the children said 'they don't really know what it's about.'

Researcher comments

Limiting the children's experience of Circle Time to this one activity, as observed in this year 1 class and in year 2, where there was less emphasis on justifying one's comment, raised some questions.

Is the experience for the 'Special Person' just tokenistic? Although the children unanimously liked being Special Person, they also sometimes found it difficult to find something good to say about the person in the middle.

It is quite hard if you don't really play with the person at all, or don't see very much of their work; some are naughty and we don't play with them and then we just try and think of something, we just say they do nice colouring or nice writing.

(Year 2 girl)

As all children are expected to say something, is there any benefit in effectively making children be positive about their peers? If what they say is not meaningful, or even true, what message does this convey to them (that adults think superficiality, insincerity or lying is acceptable)?

The development of self-esteem was cited as the school's and the two year 1 and 2 teachers' main aims in undertaking Circle Time. But it is at least arguable that accurate self-esteem relates in part to reasoned consideration (if not acceptance) of others' appraisal/criticism. What sort of personalities are developed if faults fail to be recognised personally or identified by others? Would it not be more appropriate for pupils' personal and social learning to enable them to both recognise strengths and weaknesses and how to improve them?

Further evidence from this school demonstrates the complexity of making such judgements. In terms of raising morale or self-esteem it might be justified since in interview the year 2 teacher mentioned that, although the recognised procedure was for the child who was Special Person the previous week to pick the next pupil's name out of the tin, she had 'fixed it' once so that a particular girl was picked as she was very timid, was having problems at home and needed support. 'It took a lot of doing, because the children are very quick, but it really was worth it for the beam across her face – it was lovely.'

And in the year 1 Circle Time the child whose name was selected from the tin was autistic. He and his friend were sent out of the class with the register while the class were instructed to 'think of something nice to say'. His special needs assistant was not included in the Circle Time, though she was in the room. The children made comments such as 'He has nice writing'; 'He has good cutting', 'Nice colouring in', 'I like his painting'. (Teacher: 'What have you seen? Which painting do you like?') 'He's kind and helpful'; 'I like playing with him'; 'He's always got a smile on his face.' (Teacher: 'How is he kind? Think about it and we'll come back). The boy in the middle grinned all the way through the positive comments.

Furthermore, in the opinion of the headteacher:

I feel I've learned the value of emphasising the positive side, which wasn't emphasised enough – it now has more impact and emphasis. Staff have had to learn that children don't always think positively, they can be very harsh. ... It's a fact of life, though sad, that it's hard to like some children, so it helps staff too to focus on the positive. ... Even if [Circle Time] only benefits one or two, it's worth it.

4.6 Key findings and issues

♦ Care is needed to ensure clear and shared understandings of the practical issues concerning the distinctive features of Circle Time: layout, circle formation, sitting arrangements and passing an object.

♦ Though the teacher is within the circle, she/he has a prime role with respect to the conduct of activities and pace: getting started, building structure, keeping contributions going, 'passing' (not speaking) and expectations of pupil behaviour.

♦ Pupils' participation is linked to such issues as size of the group, pupil characteristics and peer pressure or encouragement.

♦ Many teachers experience discussion or disclosure of sensitive issues with pupils, shared confidences or instances of breaches of confidentiality outside the group. Professional follow-up is sometimes required to deal with ethical concerns.

♦ Teachers cannot always articulate what accounts for their success.

♦ Drawing on observation and interview data some critical comments are made in relation to the ethos of the circle, appropriate topics for Circle Time and the modification of processes and practices.

5   Teachers' learning and perceptions

The research aimed to augment and compare the account given by school senior managers about the training which teachers had received in Circle Time by talking with teachers observed doing Circle Time and to explore these teachers' perceptions of and learning from Circle Time for themselves, their pupils and the school as a whole.

5.1   Class teachers' training

Whilst the majority of senior managers had claimed to have had some training in Circle Time, it seemed that fewer class teachers in the case study schools had.

Training may only have been available to one or a few staff in a given school, and fairly often this was very informal and consisted of 'watching others'.

> One Reception teacher had learnt by watching another teacher with whom she shared a job, but she remained conscious that her colleague might not have been undertaking Circle Time in the way intended.

> In School C, the PSE teacher had observed colleagues from a local authority 'behavioural centre' working with a boy for six weeks. This had started the school's work with Circle Time, which subsequently involved the use of well known books and videos (e.g. Bliss *et al.*, 1995; Bliss and Tetley, 1993; Mosley, 1993a) and gradually spread Circle Time to other colleagues.

In many cases the school's approach may not have been coordinated or across the school as a whole.

> For example, in School N there was interest in Circle Time and its introduction in the school to help with school ethos, behaviour and discipline. The Acting Head and year 4 tutors had been on a two-day course run by the LEA's PSHE adviser. Some teachers had concerns that they might not be able to cope with the emotional aspects of the work (dealing with the children's fears and the relationships required). These worries were not allayed by the inservice experience.

The year 6 teacher (with 31 pupils) had not received training and had no access to books. He had learnt about Circle Time from his wife, who had experience of it in initial teacher training. He aimed to use Circle Time to help with problem solving, develop communication and foster self-esteem. He felt that Circle Time had achieved these outcomes and had helped him get to know the children faster during their first term together. However, he was concerned about some of the stories told and that confidences may have been compromised. Apart from discovering informally, with some relief, from his year 4 colleagues that his approach had been broadly similar to that used in the LEA training, he had not had any opportunities to share an understanding of Circle Time strategies with them. The school intended to have an in-school staff development day.

Even in schools reported having a whole-school approach, usually only two or three teachers had received training. Some schools planned to involve other staff in training within and beyond the school. For example,

A year 5/6 teacher in School L, who had received some LEA training involving Circle Time as part of work on gender and cultural diversity, was helping to train colleagues in Circle Time.

The following case study shows how pedagogical innovation may occur where conditions are favourable:

The headteacher of School E had observed a newly qualified teacher using Circle Time with year 1 and was impressed by the results. Two other teachers had undertaken LEA training in Circle Time. One described this as 'very good and at teacher level. It gave us ideas and ways of how to use Circle Time and include stories. The trainer made me feel I knew what I was aiming for and how to be creative.' Learning the techniques and the model were most useful. The training with other teachers included experiencing Circle Time themselves so they had a sense of how pupils would feel.

The head teacher described the training as 'Very useful. It had a knock-on effect in the classroom as teachers could bring new ideas/techniques to Circle Time.' The school had purchased materials on Circle Time. Each class usually had one or two Circle Time sessions per week. The school staff shared experiences and built on what was learnt. The head intended to send other teachers on local training, which was listed in the training handbook under Teaching Strategies (not PSE) and planned to extend the training programme to the lunch-time supervisors, one of whom had seen a class Circle Time and had been 'surprised by it. I liked it more than I thought.' Another plan was to set up an evaluation process with the children and to incorporate Circle Time into structure and planning. The head thought it was important to discuss behaviour and to take time to listen, as a way of practising literacy and numeracy skills.

Occasionally teachers within a school received training from different sources, which stimulated in-school training and the move towards a whole-school approach.

In School I, one teacher had received training from a specialist in special educational needs and another from a national proponent of Circle Time. The modelling of Circle Time had been very informative, generated 'confidence and enthusiasm', and the courses had provided more access to resources. On the day of the research visit a member of the LEA Behaviour Support Team was also training a group of year 4 pupils and their teacher, a Behaviour Support Coordinator. This involved the 'Fruit Bowl' exercise (Mosley, 1993b:122; Curry and Bromfield, 1994:128), which the children soon grasped.

The training process in School K was intentionally with the whole school.

The school was linked with a local educational consultancy which provided support for developing Circle Time. The liaison officer worked in an ongoing way with the school as a whole. Thus the staff had learned to develop group identity and discuss feelings (rather than just giving news), and to be aware of strategies for support and the need to keep the contributions positive.

By contrast, in some schools teachers had received no formal training and for various reasons they often seemed to consider training unnecessary.

A year 1 teacher in School A had seen Circle Time used in a variety of forms when working as a supply teacher and had vague memories of informal guidance during one staff meeting. In her present school the headteacher and deputy head had given her a list 'of what we expect' and she had informal conversations with other teachers. It was interesting to find that, in contrast with PSE, she did not feel the need to prepare for Circle Time: 'It's the children, it's their time, it's not my time, it's what they've got to say about each other, so it's not really a preparation thing for me.'

Her year 2 colleague, concurred: 'A lot is you just read something, take it on board, a lot is just common sense.' She mentioned that the headteacher, also an Ofsted inspector, had seen Circle Time elsewhere and had suggested to staff that it be introduced 'to raise self-esteem. It was coming up to Ofsted time!' However, the headteacher claimed 'I never seek to impose style or practice – they have to feel comfortable. They've fallen into a common pattern of low key Circle Time, which has evolved.' There had been a staff meeting (including special needs assistants and classroom assistants, but not lunch supervisors) to discuss 'what we needed and could manage' of Circle Time and an 'adapted' model was adopted. The head saw Circle Time as 'part of the whole school ethos; it can't be tokenistic and it's only one part of what we do.'

One teacher, who described Circle Time as 'magical', had no training in the strategy, although she had read many books on it and discussed it at staff liaison meetings.

We skill share among language development coordinators. It has been mentioned we would like more information on this. Eventually someone who feels they have the knowledge will do some training. I don't think that you should expect teachers to do it in their first year, but they should take it on when ready, not when people say they should be doing it. It works better if people can observe good practice.

A year 5 teacher in School B explained that, although she had been using a form of Circle Time for four or five years, she had no formal training.

I have never seen it done on video or read about it. I have only just realised that I am doing 'Circle Time'. ... I probably just heard about it from classroom conversations, I can't remember. I've no resources on it and I've never done any training. I make up my own games. I didn't know there were any resources really I just do my own thing.

Only some of the staff used Circle Time: 'The special needs teacher suggests it to staff. It is gradually spreading and being taken on board as it proves useful.' But she did not feel an overriding need for training: 'It would be useful to have training but it's not a priority. ... It would be useful for the whole staff to have training together rather than individuals.'

Some proponents of Circle Time stress the importance of training, especially to observe Circle Time in practice. Although it may appear straightforward as a pedagogical tool, Circle Time holds professional and personal pitfalls for some teachers, with respect to loss of authority and disclosure. Teachers need a sense of structure within the Circle Time session and progression which requires preparation and planning, possibly to develop a thematic approach complementing PSE. Just watching another colleague or reading a manual seems inadequate professional preparation, as it leaves too much open to misinterpretation or conjecture. Ideally, too, the teacher's style in Circle Time should not be radically different from that in other classroom-based pedagogy, otherwise it may undermine pupils' openness, trust and cooperation in the group, which are essential to facilitate good Circle Time sessions.

As their confidence grows, teachers modify their techniques relating to timing the rounds, and pupil pauses, and extend or curtail Circle Time sessions according to practical circumstances or pupil needs. Teachers expressed two particular concerns: dealing with pupil sensitivities and involving reluctant pupils. They could most usefully be helped with these issues through in-school training by senior staff, in the context of other teaching and learning, behaviour and pastoral care policies and practices.

5.2 Teachers' learning through practice

Circle Time, like many other approaches to personal and social development, is essentially a dialogical method of learning which requires different techniques and roles from more didactic forms of pedagogy. But, as we have seen, class teachers engaging in Circle Time may lack formal training or experience. What do teachers learn about how to undertake Circle Time from actually engaging in it with their pupils?

From our research it seemed that the circle had a primitive appeal to teachers:

The whole technique was new to me, just using the idea of the circle. I'd always had discussions with the children and talked to them about things, but it was nice the idea of the circle and going round and taking turns.

(Year 2/3 teacher, School B)

Three Nursery teachers in School G were enthusiastic about Circle Time as a learning process which also had some effect on young children's behaviour, commenting

> *The circle is an easier way to keep them settled. I think it should go through the school, especially as all classrooms have carpets which they could use.*

> *No one's more important than anyone else in the circle. It's a good way for them to show each other things.*

> *There's not a lot of pulling hair and tapping each other as they can all see each other.*

However, they had also learned that children needed pre-social skills to form or stay in a circle.

> *When they're really bad at first you can't always get them into the circle. So you need some pre-social skills to be part of Circle Time. Some can't even sit, we have some 'little wanderers'. We don't insist they sit in the circle, if the younger kids are genuinely having a bad day. But with the older children if it's just a power thing we would be more strict.*

> (Nursery teachers, School G)

Some schools and some teachers use Circle Time spontaneously in response to problem behaviours. A few teachers expressed reservations about the possible negative effect of this approach:

> *I think my worry would be that if you use it too often, it could be a bit blasé, 'Oh we've got a problem, we're going to have a Circle Time'. It's a bit tricky. I haven't actually seen a child abuse it and there's been situations when I thought they would.*

Another teacher had learned:

> *That you can't do Circle Time cold – you have to know your group, have an understanding of what they want and need and have respect for individuals. You also should not imagine that Circle Time will necessarily solve problems.*

> (Year 5/6 teacher, School C)

Some teachers admitted having unsuccessful experiences with Circle Time, especially if class discipline was problematic. One teacher said that 'in the main' Circle Time had fulfilled what she had expected of it, but

> *I had one very tricky class and I didn't get anywhere with them. The discipline in that class was extremely bad and Circle Time was*

extremely hard to run with them because they really couldn't listen to each other. It became a bit of a battle. ... The games were fine, but going round in a circle and listening to each other, I don't think we ever managed to get round without interruptions.

(Year 2/3 teacher, School B)

Another fairly experienced Circle Time user said she had learnt that 'children are sometimes too open or too emotional'. One child had talked about a pet dying and this had provoked several children into crying.

A teacher of a year 5 group (School B) noted the need for sensitivity:

It needs careful handling. You have to be aware of the children's feelings all the time and keep on the ball. Sometimes I'll send the girls to the library and they have their own Circle Time. I don't go.

She had learned from Circle Time

How hard it is to keep quiet and stand back and let them think of answers. You know what you want the outcome to be but you mustn't press them. Usually the outcome is to keep equilibrium. Sometimes you may need to wait a while for an outcome.

Importantly complementing this view, an experienced headteacher who had long practised Circle Time, felt that she had most learnt listening skills from Circle Time. She said that teachers often wanted to 'steer children on', guiding and influencing them, but she believed that 'It's important to let the children have control. We need to believe in them.' (School J)

Another headteacher (School G) mentioned the need for awareness of and sensitivity to culturally differentiated patterns of communication. For example, he claimed somewhat stereotypically that, in his school 'Asian girls are not prone to speaking their minds and some Asian boys will not speak to or respect female teachers.' In referring to Afro-Caribbean boys he said 'quiet is not known to them; they'll share their thoughts, but not quietly' and he thought this could detract from Circle Time aims of calm reflection.

In some classes gender differences affected Circle Time, as indicated below:

In School F's Reception/year 1 class there were 20 boys and eight girls. The class teacher found that the boys were 'lively, interrupt, assert themselves and dominate. They don't realise others' needs. They need to learn to take turns.'

In School M, a year 2 teacher sometimes conducted single-sex Circle Time sessions to discuss particularly sensitive issues, for example, a bullying situation in the boys' toilets.

Sometimes Circle Time practices made teachers more aware of their own developmental needs.

An experienced teacher had learnt the need to plan and to 'mind your questions'. This was ironic given the unfortunate way in which she, somewhat nervously, began Circle Time with her mixed Reception/year 1 class: 'I've been thinking about our classes. Can you say what it's like in this class and what you liked here and where you're going to and what it will be like?' Subsequently in interview the teacher seemed to recognise the mistake of asking five year-olds four questions at once, 'I've had no training. I expect I do it all wrong.'

(School F)

A year 5/6 teacher noted that he tended to integrate Circle Time practices, such as awareness of privacy and confidentiality, into his general teaching style. The teacher reminded children about their 'special discussion' and told them not to refer to the things discussed in Circle Time in the corridor or playground.

(School H)

Circle Time requires teachers to feel comfortable about giving of themselves as persons.

The following contrasting responses were from two teachers in School J where Circle Time had been in use for a decade. A year 3 teacher, said she could not do Circle Time unless she enjoyed it because it 'exposes oneself. I am careful about what I say. I don't want to expose too much.' A year 5 teacher was aware that she was the only member of staff who no longer used Circle Time. She expressed doubts about it in terms of respecting pupils' privacy and the possible exposure of sensitive issues in a relatively small community. She preferred to work on attitudes and beliefs through RE, PSE and holding class debates. But she was also aware that Circle Time could reinforce 'the positive side and turning to each other' and that it developed listening skills. She acknowledged that it had made a difference to some children with special needs. Whilst not against Circle Time, she felt that other approaches were more appropriate and she attributed her reluctance to use it to 'my own insecurity'.

In many schools the use of Circle Time had evolved into, rather than been consciously and systematically adopted as, a whole-school approach.

For example, in School C, Circle Time had started in a unit for dyslexic children. The teacher in the unit (also the school's PSE teacher) claimed that 'the children have very low self-esteem and confidence, so we use Circle Time as a vehicle to develop these along with social and listening skills'. Initially, the school had 'a rota through which we send other children from the school into the dyslexic unit. Generally, we send in children who may benefit and also some who are well behaved as role-models.' The teachers 'choose a theme' for Circle Time (for example, cooperation) and the dozen or so children in the group can raise issues. Later she wrote a booklet on the theme for other teachers to use as lesson plans with their classes and in assemblies.

However, there had been a growing feeling that it could be counter-productive to 'pull out odd children', and that other children were missing out. So the school introduced a whole-class session for key stage 2 pupils for 30 minutes per week. According to the teacher with the larger group, they covered less, but it broadened the topics discussed and allowed more pupil feedback. The pupils themselves were aware of the different effects of the small-group Circle Time, compared with the whole-class Circle Time experiences: 'You could do more things [in the smaller group] because there wasn't as many people to go around ... ; and there wasn't as much talking as there is now; ... less disruption; ... sometimes [though], some people didn't get to go [to Circle Time] at all.'

The extent to which children with emotional and behavioural dysfunction should be involved in ordinary class Circle Time was a controversial issue in some schools.

5.3 Teachers' learning about pupils

Some teachers suggested that Circle Time afforded them an opportunity to listen to pupils in a way that they did not normally have, possibly because the dynamics of the circle and the rule of 'no talking unless holding the object', makes for concentration on one individual and 'reminds teachers of the unique value of each child'.

> *Circle Time helps because there are things I'm aware of as a teacher but I don't always make time to talk. I like having a separate slot for it. It helps me to be more attuned. Sometimes I take notes in case I forget and then I can address issues later. For example, one girl was taking the mickey.*
>
> (Year 4 teacher, School L)

A key learning experience for teachers was often identified as 'getting to know the children better' (acting headteacher, School A; PSE Coordinator School C). Three nursery teachers in School G said:

> *Since children often change classes annually in many primary schools, this could be an advantage when the teacher and class first meet.*
>
> *We learn more about the children and get to know them more intimately.*
>
> *You get to know them as a person, rather than just what they're capable of.*
>
> *We are more aware of their likes and dislikes.*
>
> *You get a picture of their home life.*

Some teachers also learned more about friendship groups from being a participant observer in Circle Time.

Another important learning outcome for some teachers concerned listening to the children 'without interference'.

> *To listen rather than talk … . You also realise how difficult the children find speaking. We all imagine that speaking and listening is so easy and it's not. It's not until you actually ask the child to speak that you realise they have problems with that and with understanding questions and answers and responses.*
>
> (Special needs teacher, School B)

A year 5 teacher in School M was 'surprised that children, who have not previously said a word, talk in Circle Time and others come out with what you don't expect', a view echoed by others. A year 2 colleague explained:

Things come out in Circle Time that wouldn't usually come out in discussions on the carpet. The structure of the circle enables children to feel secure to express their feelings. It's like a vent for their feelings to come out. ... Circle Time is very interactive. The children are facing each other and are therefore more focused. It's like an auditorium, but the children are looking at each other, not me.

Other teachers became more aware of some children's feelings and characteristics:

It's a time to stop and listen to the children, if you set it up right, they feel open enough to really share how they're feeling. It gives you an insight ... which in a busy classroom you don't always get. You can pick up comments and I think 'I must find out what they meant by that and talk to them quietly about that as well', so it gives you a bit of an insight into them from a different angle.

(Year 2/3 teacher, School B)

Circle Time has the advantage that I know I've talked to the child that day. Sometimes I learn what they fear, what frightens them and also what they like.

(Year 1/reception teacher, School F)

Some teachers were surprised about what they learnt about the children or raised their expectations of children's thinking and problem-solving skills.

Last year, when there were dreadful behaviour problems and disruptive pupils, we had a token system for good behaviour. Some got a lot more than their fair share. Some children complained it was unfair. We used Circle Time to discuss how they could resolve this. It surprised me what ideas they came up with.

(Year 5/6 teacher, School E)

Sometimes, where the use of Circle Time was a whole-school approach, senior management took an age-related developmental approach to the duration, functions and expectations of Circle Time.

Thus in School H Circle Time was seen as 'a useful way of helping them settle in' (Reception), a way of exploring bullying and discussion of class rules (middle years) and an opportunity to be still, quiet and reflective or to discuss contentious and topical issues, such as war and religion (year 5 and 6). The deputy head claimed that Circle Time 'helps to extend children's thinking', by exploring different values, thoughts and attitudes, and spoke of a growing awareness through Circle Time of the depth of children's thought and language, of the strong views which some children hold, and of their developmental maturity.

5.4 Perceptions of pupils' learning

In order to gain teachers' evaluation of the benefits of Circle Time for pupils, they were asked to select and prioritise five learning outcomes using the list drawn from the Circle Time literature:

1. promotes positive cooperation in the pupil group

2. develops self-esteem and/or self-confidence in some pupils

3. enables pupils to express themselves, especially their feelings and emotions

4. pupils respect and support one another

5. pupils suggest ways to resolve conflicts or problems

6. develops pupils' listening skills

7. fosters peer group pressure for behaviour

8. skills developed transfer to other areas of learning

9. pupils develop and clarify their own values

10. pupils contribute to school ethos and values not chosen by teachers

11. other.

Eighteen teachers of Nursery to year 6 pupils in 13 schools provided a total of 69 responses, with almost half of them giving five responses. Seven teachers ranked 'Develops self-esteem and/or self-confidence in some pupils' as the first learning outcome for pupils and five chose 'Promotes positive cooperation in the pupil group'. Only the first six items were ranked in first position by teachers.

Overall the items 'Develops self-esteem and/or self-confidence in some pupils' and 'Pupils respect and support one another' received the highest number of choices from teachers (12 each), closely followed by 'Enables pupils to express themselves, especially their feelings and emotions' (11), 'Promotes positive cooperation in the pupil group' (10) and 'Develops pupils' listening skills' (9). Although all items, except Item 10, were among teachers' choices of pupil outcomes, some were barely rated.

There was a measure of general agreement between class teachers and senior managers which clustered around the development of self-esteem, communication and social skills. There was also some overlap of the learning outcomes identified by pupils, who considered that Circle Time had helped them to learn how to listen, sort out problems, pay attention and develop ways of understanding and expressing feelings. Senior managers, class teachers and pupils shared a perception of improved communication skills, especially listening and speaking, self-esteem and self-confidence, and a cluster of other-directed attitudes and abilities concerned with respect, feelings and problem-solving.

An important rider here is that teachers' views were usually based on subjective evaluations of pupils' skills, attitudes and behaviour, not on pupils' views or scientific measures of self-esteem. Few teachers seemed to have evaluated Circle Time sessions with their pupils, although the year 5/6 teacher in School C claimed to ask pupils at the end of every half term what they had enjoyed in Circle Time 'What have I done wrong? What can we improve? What can I change?' Special needs teachers, who may be more used to reviewing behaviour and achievements also tended to review the process with their pupils (have we listened, sat well, interrupted, has anyone got upset?).

> *They enjoy it, and look forward to it. It is something different to other normal classroom activities. If they miss it or we have to cancel it they really don't like it. They also have the chance to talk about what they have learnt at the end of sessions.*
>
> (PSE coordinator, School C)

The following section uses evidence from observations, teacher accounts and in some cases, pupils' own comments, to illustrate and evaluate the pupil learning outcomes endorsed by the teachers.

5.4.1 Promotes positive cooperation in the pupil group

Cooperation

In School C, a class group of 16 girls and 19 boys in year 5/6, seated on chairs in a carpeted music room, had played a mix up game (Chair on the Right) led by the class teacher. The PSE teacher then led the circle in a question and answer session reviewing the aims of the cooperation games from the previous week. The activity was repeated to speed up the completion of a jigsaw by cooperating more effectively even though silently. There was silent applause from the class teacher for the group who finished first. Later, in reviewing the exercise, he pointed out that some groups 'didn't team' and he exhorted 'Remember, apply some of the things we've done today when you work in the classroom.' The activity was followed by a friendly 'people hunt' – to emphasise that cooperation requires communication. 'Put up your hand if you've found out something new about someone in this circle. What have you found out? The session ended with a visual and physical display of cooperation. At first two children (two girls and two boys), back to back, arms linked, on floor, had to see who could stand up without touching floor with hands. Then the exercise was repeated by four pupils (four girls and four boys), to see if a larger number of pupils made it easier. There were lots of shouts from around the circle during this exercise – 'pull her/him up', 'just pull!' and a huge cheer went up when the two groups managed to get up. The class teacher reiterated the cooperation/teamwork theme in technology (pupils were working together to design and construct a moving vehicle) and in literacy.

One pupil claimed that Circle Time 'helps you cooperate with other people better; team games.'

5.4.2 Develops self-esteem and/or self-confidence in some pupils

One child who was described as 'rarely speaking' spoke in Circle Time about his likes and dislikes. The teacher thought this was 'an enormous breakthrough'. (School J)

5.4.3 Enables pupils to express themselves, especially their feelings and emotions

Many teachers mentioned that Circle Time encourages children to express themselves.

It makes them think about what they are going to say before they open their mouths.

The quieter children are given the confidence to talk.

... you can see the obvious differences, children who usually don't speak will speak. After a couple of weeks one child, who didn't speak, started saying 'that's because I don't like speaking ...' he was actually able to express to them why he didn't like speaking. So that was a very great step forward, from a child who just wouldn't communicate, to being able to tell us why he wouldn't communicate. That's marvellous for him and for the other children to understand why he's like that. He's always going to be like that and it helps other children to understand his reaction.

(Special needs teacher, School B)

5.4.4 Pupils respect and support one another

The following example illustrates how the process of positive group cooperation and support can foster the development of self-esteem.

A headteacher related how a Circle Time activity, similar to Child of the Day, was used to raise the self-esteem of a particular child whom he described as 'malcontent'. His peers got together and found 'positive things' to say about the child. He was then presented with a book, containing their comments. The child was so touched by this that he started to cry, as he was unused to good things being said about him.

A skill like taking turns could be particularly difficult for some children with special needs to develop.

I think it helps raise self-esteem because it gives all children a chance. When they're in a circle they're aware of who's had a turn and who's not, and the children are very good at making sure that everybody takes their turn and making sure that nobody misses out. ... it gives them space and time to be listened to. It's about the only opportunity to make sure every child speaks.

(Special needs teacher, School B)

5.4.5 Pupils suggest ways to resolve conflicts or problems

Circle Time was often used in response to problems, especially problematic behaviour between pupils and sometimes could help with conflict resolution between pupils. 'Children get ideas from Circle Time, especially how things can be dealt with' (year 5 teacher, School M).

5.4.6 Develops pupils' listening skills

Learning to listen was both a condition and a key feature of participating fully in Circle Time. But from observation and teachers' remarks, it was often one of the most obviously difficult aspects of Circle Time for children to master.

> *No difficulties, only listening skills for the others* [not speakers] *and maybe little conversations going on at the other side of the circle, but they soon learn that they've got to listen.'*
>
> (Year 1 teacher, School A)

Where pupils were particularly attentive some teachers of older pupils found 'They listen really well and can respond or comment in relation to what several speakers before have said' (year 5 teacher, School M).

5.4.7 Fosters peer group pressure for behaviour

Both pupils and teachers could see and report the power of the group in the circle with respect to making them more aware of how others think and feel and specifically of their misdeeds as bullies.

> *With issues of bullying, I've actually seen children stop being the bully and start protecting the children instead. So they actually do the complete reverse. And those children are now protective to that child instead of victimising them. I was a bit worried about whether it would last, but it has lasted.*
>
> (Special needs teacher, School B)

5.4.8 Skills developed transfer to other areas of learning

> *A lot of our children have problems with turn-taking. Circle Time improves this, especially because it's a routine and they know what is expected of them and they carry it through into other conversations. They know now in a normal conversation we don't butt in.*
>
> (Special needs teacher, School B)

However, some teachers were unsure as to whether Circle Time had enabled children to develop transferable skills. She suggested that although her group of year 4 pupils had developed respect and support for one another, shown by the fact that they listened and did not talk until their turn in the group, they did not find it easy to play together.

5.4.9 Pupils develop and clarify their own values

Although it was not common for teachers to give examples of how children developed their values in Circle Time, one teacher reported that she had discussed the Gulf War and had discovered that even five-year-olds could make a significant contribution and explore their own views and values.

On the whole, teachers did not often identify negative learning outcomes or experiences for children as a result of Circle Time, but some pupils' contributions proved difficult to follow up. For example, when discussing 'How did you feel when you first came into this class?', a girl of Asian origin followed the teacher's advice to be honest, not necessarily positive, when she tellingly answered 'I was worried because I was from another country and didn't know how to get along with English people.' (year 5/6, School E). Other sensitive issues and disclosures are noted on p. 82.

5.5 Implications for the school as a whole

Are the goals individual teachers hold for Circle Time congruent across a school and in line with its other main aims for pupils' spiritual, moral, social and cultural development? If Circle Time is being undertaken by several or most of the teachers across a school, what are the effects on other teaching and learning? Are there implications for learning in other areas of the curriculum? Can schools learn from such strategies in relation to staff development and enhancing school ethos?

Headteachers were often conscious that the development of Circle Time as a whole-school strategy needed careful handling and that teachers who did not feel confident should not be pushed into using it. However, schools sometimes failed to capitalise on a teacher's interest in and informal learning about colleagues' use of Circle Time, and did not follow up with training on an individual basis or, to better effect, as a whole staff. Some teachers who had acquired 'the basics' from reading Circle Time manuals or occasionally watching other colleagues practise Circle Time, would have liked intermediate level training, so as to be able to integrate some Circle Time strategies with their other teaching and learning practices. Training for enhancing social and personal development often received scant resources and support compared with training to implement literacy or numeracy programmes.

Some schools acknowledged they were not practising a whole-school approach, indeed, it may have been a deliberate tactic on the part of some headteachers to 'develop it gradually'. Our research process itself occasionally facilitated this.

> For example, a year 5 teacher in School M claimed that the head only discovered she was doing Circle Time when she walked through the hall as it was happening. The teacher had not been aware that a year 2 teacher was also undertaking Circle Time until the head had mentioned the researchers were visiting to observe it. During one of our visits in the staff room at lunch-time two teachers expressed interest in finding out more about it.

Interview responses indicated that when several teachers used Circle Time in a school, they were often aware that there was not a consistent whole-school approach or effect. One teacher who had successfully used Circle Time in three schools said:

> *I couldn't say about this school, there are a few of us that use it but there is no consistent approach. In the school I was working in first I don't think I was there long enough to see that. I did the* [training] *course and left a year later. At my last school it wasn't consistent across the school although we tried. People did it in so many different ways. I've never seen the whole-school effect of Circle Time.*
>
> (Year 2/3 teacher, School B)

A PSE coordinator in School C acknowledged that that there were probably some wider school effects

> *... but it is difficult to pinpoint such improvements to Circle Time. Effects may been seen in assemblies when the children all raise their hands to talk about things they will have learnt in Circle Time, like listening techniques.*

The acting head in School A recognised that, although staff would like to think that Circle Time improved behaviour (less bullying, more caring, listening to one another), they could not attribute any improvements solely to the use of Circle Time. In fact it only appeared to be a small part of their positive behaviour management strategy.

However, in a few schools where Circle Time was more established and integrated into PSE as a whole, headteachers and others were beginning to recognise wider school effects, ranging from underlying changes in school ethos, such as 'Children are more able to express themselves', to the introduction of specific strategies which allowed pupils to build upon the learning outcomes of Circle Time. For example, as a result of the development of children's self-expression and confidence in Circle Time, School J had established a school council as a structured system for pupils to express their views and help create school rules. In School I Circle Time was said to help class discussion of items for the school council.

5.5.1 Parental awareness

Raising parental awareness of schools' use of Circle Time is especially sensitive given that the personal contributions and disclosures by the pupils carry implications about family life and values. However, this seems to have received little attention in the literature and in our research there appeared to have been few attempts to raise parents awareness of Circle Time as a learning strategy. Indeed, some schools may have missed opportunities to inform parents.

> *Some parents ask about our teaching methods and we do try to explain about play and its value. We don't mention Circle Time to them, though if the children were older we probably would.*
>
> (Nursery teacher, School G)

In other cases schools appear to have explicitly decided to inform parents about Circle Time.

> *... it's been done fairly discreetly, and I think that's the best way to use it really. Parents have said 'Well what is this Circle Time?', and I think it's better if it isn't announced. There has been a criticism, not from this school, about Circle Time that the parent reacted to their child's emotions almost being opened up. They resented that being public in the school ... I actually don't agree with that, but that was their opinion. You have to be careful and I've got a couple of parents where I have to be careful ... it's a very delicate area and it has to be discreet.*
>
> (Special needs teacher, School B)

On the other hand, the report of a colleague who claimed 'the whole ethos is a family school', was a little more promising.

> *None have actually approached me. Those I have approached have been positive. I don't know if they understand what goes on. Some kids are quite open to their parents, there has certainly been no negative feedback.*
>
> (Teacher, School B)

In other schools it seemed to have been left to the children to give feedback to their parents. A few children claimed they had told parents or siblings about their Circle Time experiences. One enthusiastic girl had mentioned it to her mother:

> *Circle Time is based on feelings and emotions ... I told her about Circle Time and she thought it was a good idea – you know – and there are not so many subjects or things like it and so it is that one time for you to say if something happens to you.*
>
> (Year 5 girl, School M)

The general view seemed to be that, if children talking to their parents about Circle Time raised parents' concerns, then the school would have to deal with them. A girl in School L had told her parents, who had separated, about Circle Time. The teacher had been able to reassure the parents that their separation had not been brought up in a negative way.

However, a few schools only in this case study sample were seeking the partnership of parents in this method of personal and social development of their children.

> A year 5/6 teacher talked with parents about shared concerns about their children (for example, a boy who had failed to make friends in three years) and said if they agreed that the issues could be addressed in Circle Time, he would outline the strategy with them. The class had talked about friendship in Circle Time and the pupils interviewed spontaneously mentioned that the boy now had much more attention.

> The headteacher of School I, which was in an Education Action Zone, described the local culture as 'not respectful', with little parental support. She wanted to provide 'a culture which is more tolerant and respectful and where behaviour could be modelled'. Circle Time was discussed openly at a meeting for new parents as a way of sharing problems and improving behaviour.

It was reported at a School K staff meeting that PTA representatives had observed Circle Time in the nursery. Parents had also participated in a questionnaire evaluating their awareness of Circle Time and whether their child had learned anything from participating. The school and its link organisation planned to involve a parent group who were willing to support children and also to set up a parent education class with a view to reinforcing Circle Time strategies.

5.6 Key findings and issues

♦ Compared with senior managers, class teachers reported receiving less training in Circle Time and their training was often informal, for two or three individuals, and rarely coordinated across the whole school. In some schools, teachers had experienced training from different sources. Occasionally there could be a catalyst for whole-school Circle Time training and development. Several teachers with no Circle Time training did not consider it essential. But from our observations the implementation of Circle Time could be problematic if teachers had no serious training or experience of good practice.

♦ Teachers learned through doing Circle Time and became more aware of their own pedagogical needs.

♦ Circle Time could both act as a control on young children's behaviour and be undermined by pupil indiscipline. Some teachers were concerned that it was largely used to solve problems.

♦ Teachers learned to be aware of children's feelings and to listen to them and that it is important to give the children a measure of control in the circle. They came to know their pupils as individuals, more quickly, and raised their expectations. Circle Time helped quiet and reluctant children to communicate. Overall teachers thought children improved their self-esteem and confidence, respect and support for their peers and developed communication skills from Circle Time.

♦ In terms of whole-school implications, it was difficult to determine whether school effects were attributable solely to Circle Time or to a range of approaches to personal and social learning.

♦ Only a few schools had informed or involved parents in Circle Time as part of the shared social development of the children.

6   Pupils' perceptions and learning

This chapter addresses children's understanding of and reactions to their experiences of Circle Time, and whether they felt that they learned anything from doing Circle Time.

6.1   Experiences of Circle Time: understanding and perceptions

Children were interviewed by the researchers after they had seen them in the Circle Time and/or talking with their teacher or headteacher. They all seemed very willing to talk and in some classes others had been eager to be chosen. Though our questions were adapted to the pupils' ages, not surprisingly, some of the youngest children struggled to reflect on and articulate their experiences. Their apparent honesty, especially of those who admitted to liking the 'attention getting' aspects of Circle Time, was impressive.

Most pupils were aware of the rules and the need for confidentiality – 'secrets' within the circle – and on the whole, they respected these confidences whilst reflecting on their Circle Time experiences with the researcher. They did not seem to see a conflict between the rules of Circle Time and discussion of their experiences, as they seemed to be aware that our focus was on processes, practices and perceptions. Although the observed sessions were analysed in some detail, pupils mostly spoke in general terms, without attributing views or perceptions to others. Thus, although issues were discussed that often concerned them in their everyday school life and relationships, they mostly remained true to the spirit of Circle Time by being positive in their responses and not often explicitly criticising others.

6.1.1   Understanding processes and practices

In considering children's understanding of the processes and practices of Circle Time five themes emerged from our interview data: the group context, participation, rules, privacy and confidentiality.

Group context

A sense of group identity and trust is important in terms of what can be discussed and said with confidence in Circle Time. Especially at the beginning of term, teachers had to work to develop the group as a unit through positive strategies. However, later in the year children did not uncritically accept the need for these or see their purpose clearly.

Developing group identity and trust

In School M, a year 2 Circle Time session comprised three rounds: introducing and saying something positive about the child on their left; rolling the ball across the circle to someone they did not know and saying the person's name; and reporting something kind which they had done (the teacher reminded the class how in assembly they had talked about Jesus' hands being kind). Subsequently, two of the pupils said that, although they enjoyed the ball passing activity, they did not see its point:

Researcher	Why did you like doing that?
Girl	Normally we pass it to all our friends.
Researcher	But today you were passing it to people you didn't know. Do you think it helps to get to know people better?
Girl	But I already know everyone in the class! We don't normally talk to them.

By contrast, two year 6 boys in School N were aware of the difference group bonding could make to the Circle Time experience and outcomes.

Boy One	We kind of speak about stuff like being honest about stuff and like today we spoke about what we wanted to be when we were older.
Researcher	Right, yes.
Boy One	We'll say like when we are doing bad things. They say why they did it and if they say 'because I want attention', ... well in year 5 I did it for attention, because I did, and so everyone tells the truth.
Researcher	Do you know if they don't tell the truth?
Boy One	Well it's not often they do, it is not often that they do not tell the truth, but sometimes they might, I don't know.

Boy Two	We kind of trust them to tell the truth, 'cos no one else is hearing except the class.
Boy One	Yes 'cos they are all your friends. The rest of the school might not be your friends and then they'll hear it and then they'll start picking on you, but our class they're like nearly all friends.
Researcher	So you are nearly all friends in your class. Because you have been together quite a long while haven't you?
Both boys	Yes.
Researcher	OK, so is that important?
Both boys	Yes.
Researcher	Does that make a difference to what you can say in Circle Time?
Boy One	Yes 'cos you can trust them.

Participation

There is a general issue about who participates and how and a more specific issue about who 'passes' and why.

Participation depends on being in the circle. Children were often concerned about being unable to see or hear everyone because the circle was not well formed and this often led to anxiety, especially amongst those who were keen to get attention or to keep to the rules.

> For example, a year 4 girl (School I) had become anxious because she could only see part of the teacher and those children around her. 'I told Miss and she said that she was going round and I said "Miss I can't get into the circle" and she said "Don't worry as long as I can see you."' The girl was concerned because the teacher sometimes spoke quietly and 'Cos there's two K's in the class and I might have my hand up and the other K have her hand up and I can't see if she might point to the other K and then I might start speaking 'cos I thought she meant me.'

Pupils were aware of the rules for passing and of the expectation that they would make a contribution in Circle Time.

> *Usually Mrs M does prefer it if you do say your thoughts because some people just say 'I agree' with someone when they don't really – they just don't want to share their thoughts. Because I don't think when they*

say 'I agree' with someone, they actually think exactly the same as that person.

(Year 5 girl, School M)

This sometimes contrasted with other in-class learning.

You can pass, if you haven't thought of anything yet, but the teacher comes back to you at the end. Sometimes it can be a bit annoying when you can't think about it, you just go 'Oh no!'. You're very puzzled sometimes when you can't think of something. In other classes, you're allowed to not say anything at all if you're really shy.

(Year 2 girl, School A)

There was recognition that some individual pupils found it difficult to speak in the large group because they 'Might be shy, might think some people are going to pass it around the playground' (year 3 boy, School E). 'Because you're probably embarrassed or something ... You don't know what to say, maybe ... or you want a bit more time to think' (year 6 girl and boy, School L).

Two year 4 girls in School I vividly remembered the reaction of one boy (who was said to be 'scared of school' even though he had 'a lot of friends') in the class and the teacher's response, which had surprised them:

Girl One   ... this boy, it was his first day at school and we did Circle Time first or second day, this boy, when it got on to him he said 'I don't want to do it' and [the teacher] said 'You are only allowed one pass' 'cos he passed the second time and then he started crying and he kept shouting at the teacher.

Girl Two   So he had to go in the corner and wasn't allowed to join in Circle Time.

The same girls also mentioned an incident in which another boy 'who doesn't listen to teachers' and 'bullies people in the playground' had refused to participate and had got up and thrown his chair across the circle. Although the children often spoke about their problems in the circle, this boy did not, 'he is not allowed to join in the Circle Time'. The girls 'thought it deserves him right'. Clearly circle management can be additionally demanding where children have emotional and behavioural disorders and where respect for the teacher and discipline are challenged.

Pupils seemed to be aware of who 'passed' but that, apart from some quiet pupils, the children who 'passed' usually varied from session to session. Some older pupils also had an awareness of which pupils were more likely to contribute and the dynamics of the group:

Boy One   Sometimes there's people who say more things than other people and the next time other people say more things.

Boy Two   Today like Damien and Sam were passing to each other, they had loads of questions for each other.

Researcher I thought it was quite interesting that people asked other people questions. You asked somebody a question I remember. Somebody else asked somebody a question quite a long while after they had spoken about what he was talking about. Did you notice that?

Boy One   Oh yes, Bruce when he said about science.

                                            (Year 6 boys, School N)

These pupils regularly asked questions of one another and carried the procedure over into their Circle Time activities. They also knew that the teacher used Circle Time to talk about problematic behaviour, such as not doing homework.

Rules

Many Circle Time manuals emphasise the importance of establishing and following rules in Circle Time. The cardinal rule is about one person speaking at a time. It appeared that whilst some pupils grasped and adhered to this rule, others, irrespective of age, had to be reminded. Circle Time can serve as a primary form, or reinforcement of, classroom socialisation.

Several pupils mentioned that they were annoyed when others shouted out and flouted the speaking rule of that group or that round. Two pupils aged five-and-a-half, who had been in School F for only six weeks, could explain the significance of putting one's hand up. They clearly disliked a boy who did not follow this practice and whom they found disruptive:

Boy   He shouts out, he doesn't put his hand up.

Researcher What's important about putting your hand up?

Boy   If someone else is talking and you all shouted out then no-one would hear you, if you just put your hand up Mrs S would chose you.

Researcher	Do you learn in Circle Time that you mustn't shout out, or in another lesson?
Boy	In another lesson.
Girl	And in Circle Time.

Pupils could usually list the Circle Time rules for their particular group:

Don't speak when one person is talking.

Be patient because you will get a turn.

No speaking out when somebody is talking.

Don't make fun of whatever anyone else is saying.

(Year 1 boy and girl, School F)

Don't talk if it's not your go at saying something.

Try not to say the same thing over and over again.

If you don't properly listen to people, then you just start talking, the teacher tells you 'you've got to listen to people' and once you've got the hang of Circle Time you hardly talk anymore.

(Year 2, boys and girls, School A)

Researcher	Are there any rules you have to keep?
Girl One	Not allowed to speak when some-one else is speaking. Don't say unpleasant things about someone.
Researcher	Do you think there's a reason for that?
Girl One	Because everyone will start laughing and you'll get embarrassed.
Girl Two	And the other person will get upset or hurt.

(Year 5, School E)

But some children, in a contradictory and egocentric way, quite often ignored these rules and even when pupils paid attention to one another, they still interrupted, laughed, whispered and sometimes made negative comments.

The rules of Circle Time were interpreted and reinforced in different ways by teachers.

In one year 5 group, which passed or threw a bean bag around or across the circle, one child persistently disagreed with something which was previously said and threw the bag back to the same child for an answer.

121

One girl called a boy 'annoying' and 'sad'. The boy went quiet. Another child called a pupil 'babyish'. The teacher then took the bean bag and said 'You're not allowed to be nasty'.

(Year 5, School B)

In other groups, especially if an object was not passed around the circle, the circle was likely to become a site for discussion, rather than for ordered individual turn-taking. 'She'll bring up a subject and everyone will just start speaking about it, about experiences they've had about it and I like that.' Successful Circle Time sessions need a shared understanding of the accepted processes and practices.

Privacy

It was clear that some pupils felt that they were sometimes expected to talk about things which they regarded as personal or private, such as family incidents or the health of older family members. A year 5 and 6 teacher in School D, trying to promote a discussion of respect, invited pupils to name a person whom they respected and say why. When one child asked what to do if the reason was personal, the teacher replied: 'just say what you are happy with'. Children were aware that a peer might 'pass' 'because they're too embarrassed to say it'. A Reception teacher suggested to one girl that she should think about what she would like to tell the group, even if she didn't want to say it out aloud. By contrast, some children seemed only too keen to talk about their problems and even asked 'Is it problem time yet?'

Another aspect of privacy is the rule, stressed in many Circle Time manuals, of not naming others in the group, especially when something negative like 'teasing' or 'being picked on' is at issue. This rule was not always upheld. For example, in School L in a year 5/6 Circle Time some pupils mentioned the name of another pupil accused of teasing. Pupils knew that the rule was not to name and had expected the teacher to remind them.

'Bubble Time' offered more privacy to follow up issues raised in the circle or dealing with problems on a one-to-one basis.

Last year my teacher went out and bought us a load of pegs and we had to write our name on one. And then she got a stick and a piece of big white cardboard and drew a cloud and cut it out, and stuck the cloud on. And then if we had a problem we used to put the peg on it. And it was done at register and we're reading books, silent reading. She normally looks at the thingy and one of the pegs, takes the peg and tells that person, goes up to him and goes in the reading corner with him and they put their peg back when its finished, sorted out. ... say I had a problem in the playground and pretend Sarah pushed me – but she wouldn't do anything like that – Sarah pushed me and my teacher says 'What's your problem?', I says 'Sarah pushed me over at playtime' and she would say 'Sarah come over here a minute'. But if they're in a different class she goes and tells them to get the person from the different class, and we sort out the problem and she goes back to class.

(Year 4 girl, School I)

Confidentiality

Some pupils expressed the view that clear rules concerning confidentiality 'would help if an enemy said something, not if it were a friend.' Some recognised limited, but not strict, confidentiality 'Probably they wouldn't say about anything which was really important, they would only tell their families.' But they also acknowledged that friendships at this age could be fickle and some seemed somewhat unsure as to whether confidences were broken outside the circle. Indeed, some clearly intimated that although they felt safe, respected and able to express themselves in the Circle, they might get teased in the playground about what they had revealed. Others were more sceptical in general. By comparison, some members of a group with a strong bond claimed not to be aware of a rule about confidentiality, but claimed that 'nobody would [break a circle-revealed confidence] because they'll be sensible about it'. One child also recognised the significance of keeping contributions in Circle Time positive:

Researcher	You think it's secret do you, what everybody tells in the Circle?
Girl	Well as [the teacher] said, we are all one group, we shouldn't really go round telling other people what they've said, that they don't want anybody to know about.
Researcher	Do you think anybody does go round telling afterwards?
Girl	Don't know really.
Researcher	You haven't heard anybody do it?
Girl	I hope not.
Researcher	And do you think anybody ever uses any of that information they get to be nasty to anybody else?

Girl   No, because it's all good stuff what they say, you can't really use good stuff to be nasty to somebody.

(Year 3 girl, School J)

However, one nursery nurse mentioned that she had heard two pupils telling older pupils about Circle Time.

6.1.2 Perceptions of Circle Time

Most of the pupils interviewed were positive about their Circle Time experiences. Whilst this may be a reflection of the sample chosen for interview, most of the pupils we observed in Circle Time seemed to be paying attention and enjoying the experience. They particularly liked to be able to talk and express themselves and to hear others' voices and opinions.

> *Yes, well I think it brightens the day up .... in your class you are not allowed to have conversations, but in this you are. In Circle Time you can have conversations, it is great.*

(Year 6 boy, School N)

Girl   Because I like the games – it's really fun. Its really fun seeing like all different kinds of games.

Researcher   Do you think it is just games?

Girl   No, not really, I think it's like telling us about yourselves.

(Year 4 girl, School I)

For many the sense of fun about Circle Time and the fact that it was different from other lessons were enough to commend it: 'You don't have to do writing'; 'You get about half an hour off lesson time' (Year 5/6 girls, School E).

Most pupils appreciated the games played, usually at the beginning or end of Circle Time sessions. They could describe the games quite graphically but were often unclear as to, or unaware of, their objective and seemed not to have had this explained to them, even in a debrief.

A girl and boy in year 6 described a game called 'Sausages' in which a pupil in the middle of the circle asked questions and others in the circle had to answer 'sausages' without laughing otherwise they went into the circle (see Mosley, 1996: 166). They thought the point of the game was 'To have fun with each other and to get more friendly ...',

124

'And to learn how to play nicely', 'And also if you hate each other that you get to know – not to dislike each other – to get friends again.'

(School L)

Sometimes pupils would tell pupils in other classes about Circle Time.

6.1.3 Likes and dislikes

The children readily identified their likes and dislikes with regard to Circle Time. Overall, the number of 'likes' exceeded the 'dislikes'.

Likes

Likes focused on talking and gaining attention, learning about yourself and others and having fun.

Talking and gaining attention

For those pupils who did not mind talking, Circle Time could be a distinct opportunity to contribute or even to gain attention. Three year 5/6 pupils in School C, liked talking, whereas a fourth would have preferred not to:

I like talking about animals and whatever the subject comes up as.

I like talking about things that have happened that week, like on the news.

Whatever comes up, I talk!

Some people will speak, but they'll be really shy and speak down to their toes; ... that's me!

A year 6 boy in School N said his favourite thing about Circle Time Was 'just speaking and saying what you want to say. Getting everyone's attention to know what you feel, like.

Learning about yourself and others

Some pupils whose experience of Circle Time was limited to Special Person of the Day unanimously liked this:

If you don't really know [someone] you find more things about them.

You feel nice as well when it's your go, you feel nice and relaxed because people are saying nice things about you.

If you feel you don't really know something about yourself and somebody just comes and says it, it's a nice surprise to find out something about yourself.

(Year 2 boys and girls, School A)

Children particularly differed in the extent to which they felt comfortable with bringing their home life into the school context. Whilst some were sensitive and concerned about privacy, others positively wanted to talk about their significant others and their domestic life, especially about visiting grandparents or going on holiday.

> *I like it when I have something to show or bring in from home. Like today it's my mum's birthday and I wanted to say that but I couldn't because* [Circle Time] *was about moving up classes.*
>
> (Year 2 boy, School F)

For some pupils Circle Time could be a time of some frustration. A year 4 girl in School L had brought two Greek dolls from her collection but had not been allowed to show or talk about them.

Having fun
Some pupils recognised that Circle Time could be fun and could help with learning: 'You get to do fun things you wouldn't be able to do otherwise.' 'Learning new things. It's jolly and fun.' Learning was nearly always seen in terms of personal and social, not academic, learning.

Pupils reinforced our perception that few teachers asked them what they liked or did not like about Circle Time. Some teachers reported that there was no time for evaluation. In response to a researcher's question towards the end of Circle Time 11 girls and 12 boys in year 5 in School B responded as follows:

Researcher   What do you like best about Circle Time?

Pupils   You can tell how you feel and not have anyone answer back.

You can talk and they can't answer back.

Saying things to everyone and not just to a particular person.

Its exciting and you tell the whole class.

You can talk about it and people can't go 'that's not true'.

Telling the class something so you don't have to go round loads and tell everyone.

You can disagree and people can't get mad with you.

No-one interrupts.

You can say what you feel and miss other lessons.

You can say what you hate.

126

	Mrs R can't tell us off because she hasn't got the bean bag.
	You miss lessons.
	It wastes time.
	It's not a waste of time.
	You can share feelings and emotions, but that's all for girls.
Researcher	What don't you like about Circle Time?
Pupils	If they don't agree then they wait till their turn and then start lecturing you.
	When boys talk about football and computer games.
	When some people don't say anything.
	Girls always make themselves fall out because of what they say in Circle Time.
	I get fed up with girls saying 'I haven't got any friends ...'

Dislikes

Dislikes focused on other pupils' behaviour and sometimes teaching style.

Other pupils' behaviour

Children often claimed that the worst thing about Circle Time was when 'other people spoil it.'

When you are last in turn to speak.

When you have to wait for a long time to speak, although that's good when you haven't thought of something to say.

When someone says what you were going to say.

People spoil it, like, by shouting out when it's not their go.

(Year 2, girls and boys, School A)

Sometimes you get annoyed with people.

[Others who would not cooperate in a game]

Two year 3 girls in School K added honestly:

Girl Two	When it's about me being naughty.
Girl One	When other people are being naughty and you can't get to hear other people saying things ...
Girl Two	And talking when you are speaking it is really annoying when they always talk and take absolutely no notice because that's against the rules.

127

Teacher's style

In one Circle Time, during which pupils played cooperative small group games, the PSE teacher leading the session repeatedly compared the performance of this class with that of others. One of the girls interviewed approached the researcher at the end of Circle Time and said 'When she does that, it makes us feel bad, I don't like it.'

Two girls (year 4, School K) disliked the teacher's lack of pace – 'if you don't sit properly she like stops Circle Time and tells them off' – or having to sit cross legged. They also said that it took too much time for the teacher to record comments about Child of the Day.

6.2 Learning from Circle Time

During the pupil interviews we offered pupils a list of nine possible learning outcomes, suggested by our review of the literature and asked: 'Does Circle Time help you to:

1. listen to other people?

2. pay attention?

3. sort out problems?

4. feel better about yourself?

5. think about how other people feel?

6. get to know other children?

7. say how you think and feel?

8. work better in the class?

9. make rules you can keep?'

We also asked 'Can you think of any other way Circle Time helps you? How does Circle Time help most?'

The pupils provided a total of 71 responses, with nine of the 19 interview groups making four responses each. The responses were usually worked out and agreed by the pupil 'pairs' but were not prioritised. Pupils were reluctant to say how Circle Time helped them most. This suggested, as did the analysis and number of their choices, that many pupils perceived Circle Time as helping them to learn about several aspects of personal and social interaction in the class environment. 'Listen to other people' gained the highest number of responses (14), then 'sort out problems' (10), 'pay attention' (9), 'feel better about yourself', 'think about how other people feel', and 'say how you think and feel' (8 responses each), 'get to know other children' (6), 'work better in the class' (5) and lastly 'make rules you can keep' (3).

We have used this framework of responses to illustrate pupils' accounts of their learning from Circle Time. Some accounts are quite complex and situated in the rich detail of their everyday classroom life and relationships. It is interesting to note that the learning outcomes which pupils most talked about in interview were to do with feelings and sorting out problems.

6.2.1 Listening to others and paying attention

Although 'listen to other people' gained the highest number of responses, and this item, together with 'pay attention', received around one-third of the total responses, we have no clear accounts of how precisely Circle Time helped children to do this. Perhaps this is not surprising as these were young, sometimes very young, children and many adults would have difficulty reflecting on and articulating such learning.

If asked to elaborate on their response 'It helps you to listen', children emphasised the importance of maintaining eye contact and being able to hear others in the circle.

Girl One   Feel like adult if you listen to other people.

Girl Two   Mature, yes.

Girl One   Sometimes it makes me feel like an agony aunt.

(Two year 4 girls, School K)

6.2.2 Sorting out problems

Researcher   Do you think you learn anything in Circle Time that you don't really learn in another lesson?

Girl One   Talking about other people's problems. You can't talk about them in other lessons.

129

| Girl Two | Learned more. 'Cos like people's problems like you learn more. |
| | (School I) |

Pupils of primary age are often preoccupied with peer relationships and friendship. One boy claimed that Circle Time had helped him to make up with a friend with whom he had an argument.

Boy Two	We do sort out problems definitely.
Boy One	If there's a problem between friendship … because our friend Sam … we once had an argument we called each other names but we made up in Circle Time, sorted out our problems.
Researcher	How did you make up in Circle Time?
Boy One	Well we were talking about friendship and what people don't like and then Sam said: 'well, me and Jack have had an argument today' and then we made up in front of other people, so that made me feel better.
Researcher	What, you just agreed to be friends again?
Boy One	Yes, yes and it made me feel better.
Researcher	And what happened after the Circle Time?
Boy One	We were just friends.
Researcher	You just carried on, like before?
Boy One	Yes, 'cos we shook hands in the middle time in the middle of circle.
Researcher	And was that important that you did that in front of everybody?
Boy One	Yes, 'cos it made me feel better about myself, it got like a lot off my shoulders.
	(Year 6 boys, School N)

Circle Time was used to counteract bullying and pupil discrimination as well as developing cooperation. Many pupils claimed that it had helped them:

To get to know more people.

To stop calling people names.

To stop bullying.

*Because other people say they've been upset because someone's like
bullied them.*

(Two year 5/6 girls, School E)

In School M a year 5 teacher had used Circle Time with 10-year-olds to
discuss bullying and specifically to explore a problem with leaders who
excluded some pupils when picking sports teams.

Researcher	Why did she [the teacher] want to know about who always led?
Boy One	Because sometimes people aren't allowed into the game just because one person says they're not allowed to and all the other people want them to.
Boy Two	That happens a lot.
Boy One	But since we've had Circle Time it hasn't that much in our class.
Researcher	Why do you think that is?
Boy One	Because we all know ... nobody bullies each other because they know that they can't get away with it, because somebody else is going to tell. ... And we are not as scared to go and tell Mrs M and that they're going to beat us up after school because they won't, and we know that now. But before we were scared.
Researcher	So what made you more confident then about telling Mrs M or another teacher?
Boy One	Because we have Circle Time and it just makes us more confident, what were saying and stuff.
Researcher	And were you clear before that you should tell a teacher, or has Circle Time made you clear?
Boy One	It's made us even more clear. Before this I was kind of clear, but now its even better.
Researcher	But just having this Circle Time wouldn't stop somebody beating you up afterwards, so do you think its made other people more aware?'
Boy One	We have less bullying now after Circle Time and stuff, and people don't dominate a game or anything.
Researcher	And is that just after you've done it or during the rest of the week?

131

Boy One	During the rest of the week and nobody does it now.

(Two boys, year 5, School M)

6.2.3 Feeling better about yourself

Teachers often cite raising pupils' self-esteem as a goal of Circle Time. It was fairly common for pupils to claim they had gained in self-confidence, and therefore self-esteem, by being able to speak out about being bullied.

Girl One	Well, since we've been doing Circle Time loads of people have been saying they have been bullied, and because other people have the confidence to say it, it gives me the confidence too ….
Girl Two	I think it probably makes you understand what other people feel and listen to them and think about what they are saying … Because there was one time when we first did Circle Time, which was 'Who do you think is bossy in the class?'. And some people said me and some said A and some people said other people. And you can find out what they think of you and stop doing it …
Girl One	(turning to second girl) We haven't discussed this, but I think if we talked about who … who are good friends and who are not would be good, because you could say who are good friends and if they are treating you badly then you could say that they are good friends then maybe they will think twice about what they are treating you like. Because sometimes even if you get picked on, you still like the person who is picking on you.

(Year 5, School M)

A year 6 group in School N celebrated achievement during Circle Time. The successful pupil was allowed to bring in a soft toy and a symbol of success. One girl who had won a line dance competition brought in her boots, talked about the competition and answered other pupils' questions. The teacher asked if she would do a dance, but the girl was embarrassed and declined. However, later, after addressing the questions 'What do you want to be when you grow up?' and 'What can you do to achieve this?', she put on her boots and gave an example of her dancing to the class group.

6.2.4 Think about how other people feel

Younger children especially were more likely to have learned to be more empathetic through Circle Time. 'You learn to be kind and helpful' was a fairly common comment. One year 2 boy in School M had claimed 'It stops us being mean to people ... 'cos we don't like them'.

Researcher	Do you ever play with different people at play time because you've got to know them more in Circle Time?
Boy	I sometimes play more with T and V.
Researcher	And you didn't usually?
Boy	No.
Researcher	What made you start to play with them?
Boy	I just started talking to them really.

In year 3 School E the children agreed that 'It gets you thinking about how to treat people' and emphasised the importance of talking positively and the deterrent of disclosure.

Researcher	Does Circle Time help you?
Girl	It helps you to do, like if somebody had gone up and said something rude to them, if you thought, if you just ignored them but then they said about it in Circle Time then you know that you should not do that.
Researcher	So it made you more aware of others' feelings?
All	Yeah.
Girl	Like if you were going to say something horrible to somebody you think, 'No I shouldn't say that because they'll say about it in Circle Time'.

6.2.5 Get to know other children

Sometimes Circle Time provided an opportunity to learn more about others, to 'learn what other people like and you don't learn outside Circle Time because you don't ask them or they don't tell you' and sometimes made the children feel they shared things in common:

Boy Two	It's not secrets that they tell you, but it's something you might not know personally.

Boy One	It might be something that you like and they like.
Boy Two	And then you find out that you've got something in common.
	(Year 6, School N)

Getting to know other pupils could reassure them that other children could suffer similar problems and, by sharing, to reach solutions together.

The same year 6 boys in School N agreed that they could also learn about the teacher. Joint participation in the circle could assist pupils' confidence in self-expression and could lead to their learning things in Circle Time which they did not learn in other lessons.

Boy One	Sometimes Mrs M starts off about her feelings, sometimes she expresses her feelings.
Boy Two	Like she said 'I think a friend should be somebody who likes me', that's what she feels.
Boy One	That's her opinion.
Researcher	So you're interested to know what she says?
Boys	Yes.
Researcher	Do you find that helpful sometimes?
Boy One	Yeah, because as she expresses her feelings it makes us like express our feelings more, because we feel more confident as she's done it as well. Because she's like the leader of the pack.
	(Year 5, School M)

Elsewhere others appreciated that: 'We get to know that she [their teacher] does care about what you feel like and does listen to what we are thinking.'

6.2.6 Say how you think and feel

Some pupils welcomed Circle Time as an opportunity to learn to communicate: 'You can express yourself and people listen to you'; 'When we're in Circle Time you can say the feelings you really have because they can't la ... won't laugh.' They could listen to others to think about how others feel and also so as to be able to say how they think and feel. But many of these apparently simple exchanges were complex and serious for the individuals concerned, with many personal and social dimensions, as the following example shows.

Exploring personal challenges

Interview following an observation of year 4 Circle Time, School L.

Researcher	Tell me, when you are in Circle Time, are there any times you don't like it?
Girl One	When if like [the teacher] says 'tell if you've got anything that is upsetting you' I wouldn't like to do it because it would make me think of my brother, because he's gone through a lot and when he was born he had to go into an incubator and he nearly died so that makes me think of him.

In introducing herself, Girl One (J) had said 'I have a brain damaged brother'. It transpired that he needed constant care and that the family had been involved in a lot of charitable fundraising. Whilst she could talk to her girl friends about her brother

Girl One	… a boy in my class and some of the other boys kept teasing me.
Researcher	Do you know why they did that?
Girl One	I think it's just because they don't know about it and they just think it's really funny and all that.
Girl Two	No they don't understand most of the time. If I was J then I would feel really sorry …
Researcher	Do you think if you could explain to anybody, they would understand or do you think the teacher would have to explain?
Girl One	If boys like making fun of me and all of that, I reckon the teacher would have to explain to them.
Researcher	Have you told the teacher they do this?
Girl One	She just, at home time, she was really angry with him and she said to R, you can't have golden time for about a long time now.
Researcher	Do you think it made any difference to him?
Girl One	Yes it did …
Researcher	Did she explain to him about your brother?
Girl One	Yeah, and then she said to R, 'You have to understand that her brother is really ill and she can't put up with people teasing her.'
Researcher	Did you feel a little bit better after that?
Girl One	Yeah.

Later on in the interview:

Researcher	OK. What's you're favourite thing in Circle Time?
Girl One	My favourite thing is when the ball comes to me because sometimes I've got a lot of troubles the day before then or something and I get to tell them.

Researcher	Yes, and you don't mind saying?
Girl One	No, because like now the boys understand as they are getting older so then I know they're sensible and they won't laugh at anything I'm saying.

Both girls claimed that 'Circle Time helps you … Say how you think and feel.' …

Researcher	Do you learn anything from doing Circle Time?
Girl One	Well I learned that if people don't tell like how they feel then that can't be changed, they have to tell so other people can do something to help them …
Researcher	Are there things you only learn in Circle Time?
Girl One	Well, when some people say problems.
Researcher	You don't discuss that any other time?
Girl Two	… if I thought they were really horrible and they had a load of problems and they say it then I will get to know them and then I will be nice to them and I will know what's upsetting them …
Researcher	Have you talked to anybody about Circle Time, have you told them that you do it? Have you told your Mum or Dad?
Girl One	They said 'Well it will be really good because if anybody else had any problems they, well school would be a lot more friendly and everything would be a lot more happy'.
Researcher	So they thought it would help? Yes. And do you think the teacher explained to them at all or not?
Girl One	Amm, in parents evening …when Mrs K was here a long time ago she explained to my Mum and Dad that it is very important that we do Circle Time …
Researcher	And, say if there was a new person coming to the school, like K came, and you knew they were going to do Circle Time, what do you think would be really important for them to know about it?
Girl One	That everybody is like really important so everybody should be treated the same and nobody teased and all that.
Researcher	Does it make a difference to sit in the Circle to learn that?
Girl One	Yeah.
Researcher	How is that?
Girl One	Because then everybody will understand your problems and everything in the classroom and all that and everybody will like get along and then you can go all over the stuff that people don't understand.

It appears that the experience of Circle Time, as part of a raft of PSE and anti-bullying strategies, had enabled Girl One to talk more about what she had to cope with and had helped others to understand more.

The following conversation indicates that Circle Time could offer security and opportunity to express personal views, knowing that they had to be taken seriously and respected by others, at least in that environment.

Revealing beliefs and values

An interview with four year 5/6 pupils (School H, two girls, two boys) revealed some complex perceptions and dislikes. The pupils made comparisons between talking about beliefs and values in RE and in Circle Time. They agreed that in Circle Time it was easier to talk about feelings and, although you might subsequently get teased about what you had said in the playground, the most important thing was that people could not laugh at you in the Circle Time.

Researcher	Are there any times when you don't like Circle Time?
Boy One	When it's a boring subject.
Researcher	What is a boring subject?
Boy Two	Religion. We were talking about what's wrong with being a different religion ...
Girl One	If you can't think of anything to say ...
Boy Two	When it's like something open, like interesting, like the catching of animals or something ... it's OK.
Girl One	Religion, it's not an everyday subject.
Boy Two	So you're not like familiar with it.
Researcher	Does it [talking about religion in Circle Time] make you think more?
Boy Two	It makes you think more but you still don't know what to say.
Girl One	You knew more about it, so you had a better feeling about it after you've done it.
Researcher	Had you also talked about different religions in Religious Education?
All	Yes.
Researcher	Does that help?
Boy Two	It helps you more to understand like if you didn't understand it before, so the penny drops.
Researcher	Had you in RE talked about respecting other people's beliefs?
All	Yes.

Researcher	Was it different in Circle Time?
All	Yes.
Girl One	Because you speak to it in more detail in Circle Time.
Boy One	Because you feel like ... in RE sometimes you feel like you don't want to talk about it if you believe something – because I'm not a Christian.
Researcher	What do you believe?
Boy One	We're Bahai's and everyone else in the school is Christian or Jehovah Witness.
Researcher	So did you talk about being a Bahai in RE?
Boy One	Yes.
Boy Two	Sometimes we do RE and, say like when we have Xmas, Mr P might ask [name] 'What celebration do you have?'
Researcher	And did you feel OK about that?
Girl One	If we are all in RE then you might not want to say anything about your feelings, like 'Oh I think that's wrong because'. But if Mr P says something in Circle Time and you disagree then you can like put your hand out.
Researcher	So it's easier to do it in Circle Time?
Girl One	In RE ... you might be embarrassed about your friends, if you say like 'I go to church', then somebody might like laugh at you.
Girl Two	And start making fun of you in the playground.
Boy One	Circle Time is the easier way to express your feelings.
Researcher	But you do RE with Mr P also do you?
All	Yes.
Researcher	OK that's very interesting, and when you talk in Circle Time do you have rules about it, do you understand what people say in Circle Time might be special?
Boy Two	We have to keep it a secret what they say.
Researcher	Is that what you all know that you're not supposed to tease people?
Girl One	If like in Circle Time you say something and then in the playground you go out and play and they laugh at you.
Boy One	You're not encouraged to do that you're encouraged not to do that.

It is important to note that after this episode Girl One said the most important thing about Circle Time was that 'You can speak and no one will laugh at you.' And for Boy One it was 'What you say is private and they won't spread it around.'

6.2.7 Work better in the class

The main aim of the teacher of a merged year 5/6 class in School E was to promote cooperation, and emphasised this in the preparatory and closing activities. In one round, 'This is my classroom and in it there is …' pupils had to repeat what had been said before and add something. As it became increasingly difficult, the list was not repeated in the right order, even with sotto voce encouragement by those with the best memories. Towards the end of the round the group really helped one boy (with special needs) as all wanted him to get through the list. The teacher commented that she was really impressed by their memory and helping each other, 'so that between us we managed to get there'. The teacher claimed that Circle Time helped to achieve her aim and that pupil support through whispering and encouragement was more important than implementing the rules rigorously.

A few examples were noted of pupils transferring their learning from Circle Time to other learning, but one group of year 5/6 pupils thought that Circle Time had helped with English: 'Once we were talking about animal cruelty … and next day in English we were talking about fox hunting, so you already knew a little bit about it.'

6.2.8 Make rules you can keep

Some Circle Time sessions were used to make or reinforce class or school rules or procedures.

One year 6 girl in School L had been surprised by some things said in Circle Time

> *Sometimes like when we're playing and then in Circle Time they like say someone teased them really bad and they've got a bad cut or something then I didn't know about that and that's sort of surprising to hear.*

She reported that she had learned that 'if someone is bullying you like not to hit them back, just walk away or if they still bully you just tell Miss, not like get in an argument about it' and that, although pupils learned this in other lessons, it was clearer and had more impact in Circle Time.

6.2.9 Overview

At the end of the summer term the year 5 teacher in School M, whose class we had seen twice, organised an evaluative debrief session of their Circle Time experience. This response of one class group reflects many of the views and opinions of their Circle Time peers elsewhere.

A debrief on the value of Circle Time

Teacher   Circle Time is good for … ?

Pupils   If there's any trouble you can do what people suggest.

You get to know people's problems and how they feel.

It's not good if you're not confident.

It's helped me to show my emotions.

You can hear others' ideas if you've got problems.

If you don't want to share problems you don't have to.

If someone has been bullied you can talk about it, what you should do and what you do do.

Finding out what people think of you and other people.

Teacher   If you were doing Circle Time next year what would you personally like to discuss?

Pupils   People picking on you.

Friends and how to make them.

Bullying and how to catch them.

What tables to be on.

The playground and what happens when teachers aren't there.

If there are some things people don't agree with or they are distracting.

We should do Circle Time in the playground.

What upsets people leaving school.

Teacher   Should there be timetable time for Circle Time?

Pupil responses were divided on this. Some wanted it spontaneously: 'Only when there's a problem, otherwise it's boring' (six girls). 'When there's a bit of spare time.' Some wanted it every week: 'It's an opportunity to hear people's suggestions about your problems.' Some said fortnightly 'because everyone has a problem at some time.'

6.3 Key findings and issues

The children interviewed spoke of their experiences, perceptions of and learning from Circle Time.

- ◆ Children identified as important the group context of learning and their sense of trust in it. They had some practical concerns about being able to participate in Circle Time and recognised the challenges for some of their peers. Children were well aware of the rules and disliked those who flouted them, even though they also did so themselves. Views about what was 'personal' and the boundaries of privacy and confidentiality in the group differed.

- ◆ Interviewed pupils' perceptions of Circle Time were largely positive. They liked talking and gaining attention, learning about themselves and others, and having fun in the circle. Dislikes centred on other pupils' behaviour and sometimes on the way in which the Circle Time was conducted.

- ◆ Identified learning outcomes, particularly learning about and expressing feelings and solving problems, testify to some powerful and memorable personal and social learning.

7 Conclusions and recommendations

This final chapter comprises two separate but interrelated parts. The first consists of practical guidelines, based on the research findings, for schools and teachers implementing and undertaking Circle Time. The second is an evaluative overview of Circle Time as a strategy in whole-school personal, social and citizenship education policy and practice.

7.1 Guidelines for practice

As a result of the survey and case study research, some guidelines are offered for schools wishing to implement Circle Time or to review their practices. Guidance is also available in the main manuals and handbooks (Bliss and Tetley, 1993; Bliss, Robinson and Maines, 1995; Curry and Bromfield, 1994, 1998; Mosley, 1993a, 1996; White, 1991, 1998a and b).

7.1.1 Provision and practice

Spontaneous or planned provision?
A known and designated weekly time for Circle Time can help in delivering a planned and integrated approach as part of PSE, especially when linked with other behavioural support strategies and celebration of success in whole-school assembly. On the other hand, spontaneous use of Circle Time appears effective if used as part of a problem-centred approach, for example, in relation to playground incidents, as it capitalises on the teachable moment and can also respond to pupils' requests. Whether and how Circle Time is timetabled may have implications for its status with staff and its standing for pupils. The benefits of Circle Time may be had from either, or perhaps both, the rhythm and routine of an allotted time and the experimental and relevant feel of ad hoc provision.

Forming the circle
From the outset, attention needs to be paid to the formation of the circle as the most fundamental organisational principle in this teaching and learning strategy. Pupils placed great weight on being able to maintain eye contact and hear each other in the circle, not just to facilitate active

142

listening but also to indicate social equality. Space and place were significant contributory environmental features; a quiet comfortable room or space prevented interruption, maximised privacy and offered security.

Class size

Observations and manuals indicate that class size can seriously affect the efficacy of Circle Time. To sustain pupils' interest and participation in the round and forum the group size should not be more than 20 pupils. Teachers need to give constructive thought as to how groups can be reduced in size, for example by working with circles within circles, circles in different parts of a room or hall, gender-based groups, by eye colour and so on.

7.1.2 Teacher preparation

The teacher's role

Much of the potential for success or failure of Circle Time lies with the skills of the teacher as an enabler of communication and interaction. Although Circle Time is intended to be exploratory and democratic, teachers often intervene and dominate, rather than facilitating the discussion. Training and experiencing the feeling of being a participant in the circle helps teachers to learn appropriate behaviour in the circle and to take a back seat. Teachers need more opportunities to observe one another's Circle Time sessions, to become aware of age-related sensitivities and to develop greater coherence in practice across the school and pupil's experience of Circle Time.

Can all teachers do Circle Time?

Teachers have varying styles of teaching, reflecting their training and personalities, as well as the conditions of the class and classroom. Circle Time is a specific and structured technique, which depends on certain conditions and rules, though in outline it may be possible to adapt it to teaching and learning in other areas of the curriculum. Most importantly, it requires the teacher to engage as a participant, although as a first among equals, in the circle. The teacher is thus the conductor and facilitator of the Circle Time structure and guardian of the procedural rules, but relinquishes some control over the content of the discussion and the nature of the contributions to the responsibility of the pupils. Teachers who have a more authoritarian style or who may not feel at ease with making personal contributions in the circle group may not enjoy this style of teaching and learning. Teachers who are themselves prepared to learn from using Circle Time may realise it has wider and deeper implications for their practices. For these reasons, teachers should not be pressurised into adopting Circle Time just so that a school can claim it is a whole-school practice.

Preparation and evaluation

As with any other teaching and learning strategy, enjoyable and effective Circle Time needs thoughtful preparation so that the teacher can avoid personal sensitivities for pupils, capitalise on burning issues and ensure that the Circle Time experiences are appropriate and enjoyable and learning outcomes progressive. Experienced Circle Time leaders can modify recommended procedures and practices to meet the differentiated needs of their group, whilst not compromising on the pedagogical underpinnings or the way in which content fits with other appropriate learning. Pupils need to be informed about the objectives of Circle Time so that they see it as learning and not merely talk or play. Evaluation with the children can provide feedback to reintegrate into preparation. Teachers need to take time to reflect on their practices in some detail: what was done and why, what worked or did not work, when, where, with whom and why?

7.1.3 Ethical concerns

Participation and non-participation

In Circle Time, the degree of individual contributions to discussion is evident to all. The teacher's handling of inappropriate or excessive contributions or of a child who always 'passes' gives signals to the group. Since Circle Time requires social and linguistic skills, participation may be particularly difficult for pupils who do not have English as their first language and are still learning communicative competence, or for children with emotional and behavioural difficulties who are integrated within the circle. Pupil partnerships may be established to facilitate voicing of contributions. A consistent approach to the rules for participation and inclusion is important. Teachers should not try to psychoanalyse pupils. Teachers should encourage children to speak but recognise that not all children will improve their self-esteem through having attention focused on them. Some may feel threatened and not being able to speak in the circle may tend initially to lower their self-esteem.

Sensitivity, confidentiality and disclosure

A sense of belonging to and trust in the group are essential to the underlying ethos of the Circle Time experience and rules of anonymity, cooperation and non-disclosure beyond the group cannot be stressed enough. Pupils are expected to reveal their personal thoughts and feelings and address concerns and issues of social interaction in the circle. Such discussions may involve sensitive interpersonal psychological and physical responses. Serious matters of bullying and racial harassment may be too sensitive for disclosure in an open forum, the more so because a group environment in which such behaviour occurs may undermine the level of trust and confidentiality needed for victim and perpetrator to confront one another. A suggestion box could allow issues to be raised anonymously. Some activities in the circle can also provoke personally and culturally differentiated responses.

Parental awareness and involvement

The school, teachers and peers are certainly not the only (or even the most significant) personal, social and civic educators. By the primary phase children have already developed culturally conditioned moral and social attitudes and behaviours. Although primary schools are generally perceived as promoting more parental liaison and interaction than secondary schools, they vary in the degree to which they operate in partnership with parents. This was evident in schools' efforts to raise parents' awareness of Circle Time. It is perhaps not surprising, but paradoxical, that schools are often cautious about informing and involving parents in their child's personal and social education. This may confront the child with the need to make sense of potentially different values, attitudes and behaviours between school and home life. Schools need to develop clear, coherent and shared PSE policies and practices, including Circle Time, to give teachers confidence to involve parents in personal and social education partnerships which can support and reinforce positive Circle Time strategies.

7.1.4 Intentions and perceptions

Matching aims with outcomes

Social and personal learning often need more self-conscious reflection and willingness to learn from negative experiences than cognitive learning does (for example, in the literacy or numeracy hours). Although class

145

teachers were able to state their aims to researchers, they did not explicitly communicate these to pupils and they rarely evaluated the Circle Time experience or debriefed the children. As with other learning, it should be possible for teachers to be more explicit about the purposes and the moral ground rules of Circle Time (such as respect for others in turn taking and active listening, equality within the group, cooperative problem solving) and the expected learning outcomes of some rounds and activities. In this way, they would facilitate pupils' reflection on their responses and experiences and monitoring of their social and personal development.

Ensuring equal involvement
Group activities are a way of defusing tension from the open forum and introducing variety into learning. However, some pupils benefit more than others from games and complimentary exchanges. Teachers need to ensure that children are not excluded or suffering a lowering of self-esteem. Even a seemingly pleasant discussion of forthcoming holidays can demoralise those children whose situation contrasts with that of the majority. Teachers need to scrutinise their sessions to develop peer group support and to maximise the opportunities to meet the Circle Time goals and to minimise any implicitly negative effects.

Individual and group progression
Group work has to pay attention to both individual and group learning. Circle Time emphasises socially mediated learning and the development of participative skills in the round, open forum and other activities. Greater attention is needed to ensure that pupils relate to and build upon one another's contributions rather than producing a series of monologues. The latter only satisfies minimal conditions of communication and participation, whereas there is exponential scope to add to and develop ideas, expressions of feeling, solutions to problems and so on. Further thought should be given to learning progression so that Circle Time does not simply repeat the same rounds or celebrate success through an institutionalised 'special person of the day'. The more effective Circle Times were part of a carefully structured and thematically crafted PSE programme which paid attention to the development of specific values or virtues over several weeks or half a term.

7.2 Circle Time as a strategy in whole-school PSE and citizenship policy and practice

As we have seen, many claims have been made for the power of the circle and groupwork. However, Circle Time seems to lack an agreed and commonly understood definition, structure, content and processes. It is characterised by diversity in implementation, although it has groupwork in a circle at its core. Proponents and trainers have noted its positive potential, but this requires preparation, planning and implementation into schools with at least a minimally supportive climate of recognition and encouragement as well as established behaviour management practices.

Primary schools perceived the introduction of literacy and numeracy hours at the end of the 1990s as reducing the time available for Circle Time, except where it was already well integrated with teaching and learning and PSE practices. However, since 2000, the stress on delivering Citizenship Education, alongside PSE, offers primary schools an additional justification for Circle Time.

The examples of Circle Time objectives, provision and practice (see Chapters 3 and 4), illustrate a more democratic and egalitarian approach to teaching and learning. When it works well, Circle Time offers a forum in which pupils and teachers share responsibility for finding and implementing ways of dealing with problems identified by individuals and the group.

7.2.1 What are the implications of Circle Time for whole-school development and training?

Proponents and trainers emphasise that Circle Time should fit in with other PSHE and citizenship developments, assemblies, work with governors, visitors, extra-curricular and lunchtime experiences and so on. Teachers' aims vary according to the age, academic and social abilities of the children in the group and the learning environment. Further evaluative work should clarify the best strategies to develop specific skills, qualities and characteristics, so that schools may make informed choices about complementary approaches, such as Philosophy for Children, Just Communities and School Councils. Schools may need to undergo a curriculum audit and mesh this with an analysis of learning opportunities for developing personal, social and civic knowledge, skills, understanding, values, attitudes and characteristics.

7.2.2 What precisely can Circle Time contribute?

Circle Time, like some other active learning strategies, lacks theoretical grounding. What is distinctive about Circle Time that brings about the positive outcomes which are claimed for it (group belonging, caring, problem solving, the development of personal, social and communication skills, and self-esteem and confidence)? Should specific features – the circle format with everyone at the same level and the specific rules and structure – mean that Circle Time, rather than other techniques, should be used to deal with certain issues in PSE? Are teachers and student teachers sufficiently skilled in conducting activities and discussions in a circle? Our observations and the concerns of proponents and trainers, suggest that some teachers have only a superficial understanding of Circle Time pedagogy and that its apparent simplicity can lead to cosmetic implementations of some Circle Time activities (e.g. Special Person of the Day). Appropriate training and opportunities to observe and experience Circle Time practices, together with ongoing professional sharing of and reflection on experiences, are essential if the ideas and processes are not to become diluted and even damaging. More evidence is also required to demonstrate more precisely how those teachers who have experienced training, or training from particular proponents, practice Circle Time and how this differs from that of teachers who have no direct training experience.

There is still inadequate research to support respondents' claims made for Circle Time and the perceptions of pupil learning outcomes reported above (for example, enhanced self-esteem). A few well-conceived and executed intervention studies utilising a matched control group and appropriate assessment measures of self-esteem and other attitudes and abilities could go some way to providing further, quantitative support. On the other hand, the strength of Circle Time as a pedagogical tool may lie partly in its motivational force, in that its processes contrast with other learning techniques and that most students find it enjoyable and fun. Public acknowledgement and peer encouragement in the circle can be powerful motivators for change. Important experiences and evidence of learning include pupils' reports that listening in the circle to another child's expression of feelings about being bullied has made them think again about their behaviour, or their demonstrations in the group that they are able to offer criticisms in a positive way.

There is, as yet, no clear evidence of sustained, progressive and transferable learning from Circle Time to other curriculum areas. Claims that Circle Time can enhance academic performance, especially through increased self-esteem, self-confidence and communication skills are also unproven. Is the promotion of self-esteem, respect for self and others due to Circle Time, or to a focus on these values and qualities as part of wider pedagogic practices and a whole-school approach to PSE and citizenship?

Benefits for teachers are rarely stressed by advocates of Circle Time. For many teachers, the Circle Time pedagogy represents a change from their usual teaching and learning methods. They derive satisfaction from children's enjoyment and gain new insights into their pupils, which may help interpret their responses in other learning contexts. Moreover, a common involvement of teachers in Circle Time may make for greater staff interaction at all levels in sharing teaching and learning experiences and support.

Circle Time challenges teachers and pupils to be open about themselves, to add a personal perspective to their class learning and to recognise one another as learners and individuals. This may empower pupils and blur the personal and professional boundaries of the teacher and influence perceptions of the teacher as both an authority and in authority. Good teaching is grounded in and works with relationships for learning. Circle Time is a teaching and learning strategy which requires personal and emotional investment on the part of the teacher and pupil, without compromising on values, virtues and cognitive abilities. Through this strategy teachers and pupils may be learning together.

As an active learning strategy, Circle Time can promote learning to become a good moral citizen through opportunities to develop listening and speaking skills, personal and social awareness, practising respect, participation and expression of feeling, as well as gaining increased knowledge and understanding. Engagement with Circle Time processes may, in turn, require a reappraisal of the role, authority and practices of the teacher, redefining relations of power and control. Enabling students to become moral citizens may make them more likely to challenge the traditional patterns of learning, teaching and decision making in the school to make them more transparent and democratic. The way in which the school responds is indicative of its role as a moral, social and communicative institution. Circle Time could be a strategic dimension in developing a transformational pedagogy and a teacher, pupil and parent partnership in personal, social and citizenship learning.

Appendix 1 Research methodology

The research comprised five main processes:

1. a review of the literature on Circle Time

2. telephone and face to face interviews with proponents and trainers of Circle Time

3. sampling a research database

4. telephone interviews with headteachers and coordinators in schools undertaking Circle Time

5. visits to case study schools to carry out observations of Circle Time sessions and interviews with teachers and pupils.

Literature review

A search of the research literature on Circle Time which had been undertaken for a critical review of research on values, attitudes and personal qualities for Ofsted in 1996 (Halstead and Taylor, 2000) was updated specifically for this project and reviewed again when writing this report. In addition, a search of publishers' catalogues and databases was made to compile a list of curriculum resources for teachers directly related to Circle Time.

Drawing on the available literature, Chapter 1 gives a description of Circle Time, its origins, practices, aims and claims made for it. The literature review was used to identify the issues and the questions for: interviews with the proponents of and trainers in Circle Time techniques and the headteachers interviewed by phone (Chapter 2); the Circle Time experiences observed; interviews and discussions with the teachers (Chapters 3, 4 and 5); and pupils (Chapter 6) in the schools visited. A full bibliography is provided.

Contacts with proponents and trainers

We contacted many proponents and exponents of Circle Time and attended a national conference on Quality Circle Time – the heart of the curriculum, at which one key exponent gave a public demonstration (Antidote, 1998; Reed, 1998). We conducted telephone interviews with eight Circle Time proponents and visited two key exponents (see Chapter 2). Those interviewed included three of the foremost exponents of Circle Time who have each written several books for teachers on how to use the strategy and who also provide training for teachers. Other interviewees included LEA trainers; health education trainers; those working in colleges of teacher education; trainers in voluntary organisations for young people and parents and those working in therapeutic group work, especially in circles, with children and teachers. The ten interviews covered a common core of questions, oriented to suit the particular role and, if known, the approaches and principles of the trainer. Topics included: the interviewee's background and involvement with Circle Time; the theoretical basis of Circle Time; specific emphases of Circle Time in their approach; the outcomes and benefits of, and concerns about using Circle Time in schools; contacts with other organisations using Circle Time.

Using the database and sampling

Using an existing NFER database of schools which had responded to a previous national survey of values education (Taylor, 2000: 163), a sample was compiled of 100 schools using Circle Time and which were nationally representative of school type, geographical region and range of student academic ability.

Researchers conducted 57 telephone interviews (out of 100 schools). Forty of these involved senior managers (34 headteachers, four acting heads and two deputy heads) and the remainder involved two PSE coordinators, three SEN coordinators, one key stage 1 coordinator, a Section 11 teacher, five nursery and infant teachers and five key stage 2 teachers. Of the 43 schools which declined to participate in the research, five claimed that they no longer used Circle Time (in one case because classes were too large), five had no knowledge of doing it in the past and five had not 'got it off the ground'. In 18 schools it was not possible to contact the headteacher and 10 headteachers declined to be interviewed because they were 'too busy'.

Telephone interviews

Table 1 cites the characteristics of the 57 schools as defined by the initial questionnaire respondent, with whom a telephone interview was subsequently conducted.

Table 1 Overview of the characteristics of the 57 schools telephoned about Circle Time

Pupil numbers (49–461)	1–100	101–200	201–300	301–400	401+	
	6	21	21	6	3	

Main catchment	Inner city	Urban	Suburban	Small/med town	Rural	
Schools	9	12	10	12	14	

Ability	High	Low	Middle	Few High	Range	NR
Schools	5	10	14	3	23	2

Proportion receiving free school meals	<10	10–25	25–40	40–55	55+	NR
Schools	17	20	6	6	7	1

Ethnic minority pupils	<10	10–25	25–40	40–55	55+	NR
Schools	46	3	2	0	6	

The telephone interview schedule included questions about:

- why and for how long Circle Time had been used
- aims and whether these were shared by staff
- how many staff used Circle Time and in what circumstances
- the amount and usefulness of Circle Time training
- the year groups involved and duration of Circle Time
- learning outcomes for pupils and teachers
- wider school effects
- plans to continue to use Circle Time.

The findings are given in Chapter 2.

School visits

The 14 case studies were intended to provide qualitative findings from observation of examples of positive practice and discussion of issues associated with successful and also less successful experiences of Circle Time from the perspective of pupils and teachers. The characteristics of the 14 case study schools (Table 2) were broadly similar to those of the 57 schools with which telephone interviews were conducted. They were chosen because they provided evidence of one or more of:

- a purpose and plan for using Circle Time

- training

- integrating Circle Time as part of the school's personal and social development practices

- making some clear claims about learning outcomes.

Schools were included which had used Circle Time for different lengths of time and we aimed, where possible, to observe and interview pupils of a younger and an older age group.

Table 2   Overview of the characteristics of the 14 case study schools

Pupil numbers (125–419)	1–100	101–200	201–300	301–400	401+
	0	6	6	1	1

Main catchment	Inner city	Urban	Suburban	Small/med town	Rural
Schools	2	3	5	0	4

Ability	High	Low	Middle	Few High	Range
Schools	2	2	1	1	8

Proportion receiving free school meals	<10	10–25	25–40	40–55	55+
Schools	5	6	2	0	1

Ethnic minority pupils	<10	10–25	25–40	40–55	55+
Schools	12	1	0	0	1

Case study schools represented the complete range of school type (see Table 3):

- eight infant/junior schools, two junior schools, two infant schools and two first schools
- five schools were denominational (Church of England)
- schools were located in a wide geographical spread across England
- catchments ranged between suburban, rural and urban/inner city
- size ranged from 125–419 pupils, the majority having between 125–293 pupils
- most schools catered for the full range of academic ability, but two classified themselves as having an overall tendency towards high academic ability and two as having an overall tendency towards low academic ability
- with the exception of School G, most schools had fewer than one in ten pupils of minority ethnic origin
- except in School G, the proportion of children receiving free school meals was mostly lower than one quarter.

Seven of the 14 schools (School B, D, F, G, H, K and M) were visited by two researchers, who both made Circle Time observations and notes on teacher interviews. This maximised opportunities to observe both the content and processes of the sessions and the triangulation of some data.

Day visits were undertaken over two terms to conduct a common programme of research activities, wherever possible. The aims were to:

- observe Circle Time in at least two classes
- interview the class teachers who conducted the Circle Time
- interview two or three pupils from each class group
- interview a member of the senior management
- collect relevant documentation.

Further information about the interview and observation schedules may be available on request.

Table 3   Key characteristics of the 14 case study schools

School	Age range	Location	Pupil Nos	Ethnic minority pupils %	Ability	Main catchment	Free school meals %
A	3–7	North West	185	<10	high	suburban	25–40
B	4–12	South Central	293	<10	range	rural	<10
C	4–11	North West	367	<10	range	urban	10–25
D	4–11	South Central	136	<10	few high ability	suburban	10–25
E	4–11	East	166	<10	range	suburban	<10
F	5–9	W of London	238	<10	middle	suburban	10–25
G	3–7	Central	270	>55	low	inner city	>55
H	4–11	South	125	<10	range	rural	<10
I	7–11	East	206	<10	low	urban	25–40
J	3–11	North West	227	<10	range	rural	<10
K	3–9	Central	194	10–25	range	inner city	10–25
L	4–11	East	135	< 10	range	rural	10–25
M	4–11	South Central	224	< 10	high	suburban	<10
N	7–11	North West	419	< 10	range	urban	10–25

Further descriptions of the case study schools are given in Appendix 2.

Collection of documentation

Items such as:

- school prospectus
- Personal Social Health Education Policy
- Spiritual, Moral, Social and Cultural Development Policy
- mission statement/values statement/school aims
- behaviour/discipline policy
- any documents on Circle Time
- Ofsted reports.

Eleven prospectuses (the remainder were under review) and a range of other relevant documentation was obtained (see Table 4), in particular policies relating to behaviour and discipline and PSE. Nine Ofsted reports were also obtained, from the school or the internet, about inspections which had taken place in the 18 months prior to the case study visits.

Interviews with headteacher, deputy headteacher and/or Personal and Social Education Coordinator

These covered the role of Circle Time in policy and practice in a whole-school approach to PSE; the use of Circle Time and training; the involvement of support staff and parents and the benefits, challenges and learning outcomes of using Circle Time. Seven headteachers were (re)interviewed during the school visits. A range of other senior staff, such as deputy heads, PSE and SEN coordinators were also interviewed, as well as two teachers who had been responsible for introducing others to Circle Time in the school.

Observation of two Circle Time experiences

Where possible, these were with a younger and an older age group. Some time was spent in class so that the pupils would have seen the researchers before Circle Time and to compare the teacher's style in both contexts. An observation schedule aimed to record and describe the events (content) and the processes (form) of Circle Time. Also recorded were: pupil and classroom characteristics; teacher style; pupil and circle management; use of resources; teacher-pupil and pupil-pupil interactions and pupil reactions. During the observation, two (occasionally more) pupils were identified for subsequent interview. Researchers observed 27 Circle Time sessions with nursery to year 6 groups. No age group predominated. The teachers were selected by their heads and were willing to be observed and available on the date of visit.

Pupil interview paired with a friend

The selected pupil was invited to talk about his or her experiences of Circle Time with a friend for 30–45 minutes, according to the age of the pupil and the length of lesson time available. Questions covered the timing, location and processes of Circle Time; likes and dislikes about Circle Time; whether Circle Time was helpful and if so, in what way;

learning from Circle Time and extent of enthusiasm for Circle Time. It was necessary to ensure that these young pupils appeared to understand that the interview was confidential (explained as 'No one else in school will know what you tell me.') and anonymous ('If you tell me something interesting then I might include it in my writing, but I'll give you another name.'), and that they could understand the questions and read the chart. The confidence to speak clearly and attention span were sometimes issues with younger pupils. The children were sometimes more interested in communicating with their friend. Interviews were tape-recorded and subsequently fully transcribed for analysis. We conducted 23 separate interviews in 12 schools, with a total of 35 girls and 26 boys, spanning the full age range. In two schools, it was unfortunately not possible to undertake pupil interviews (see Table 4). The greater number of girls occurred mainly in year 3 and 4. Most of the interviews were 'paired with a friend' but in seven of the interviews there were three or four pupils present.

Interview with the class teachers

These were undertaken, if possible, immediately after the Circle Time event, to serve as a debriefing experience with the teacher and to check on certain aspects of the observation. The interview covered use of Circle Time, the reasons for using it and whether this was formal or informal; cross-curricular links (e.g. literacy, music); aims for using Circle Time; theoretical awareness; training and its perceived usefulness; pupils' learning from Circle Time; evaluation of Circle Time; and teacher learning from Circle Time. The interview included two charts which attempted to force the teachers to choose three main aims and up to five outcomes of Circle Time; these items were selected from the literature on Circle Time and the claims of its proponents. Researchers interviewed 28 teachers, all of whom had been observed conducting Circle Time sessions. In one school no teachers could be interviewed because it was too close to the end of term.

Table 4 Research programme in the 14 case-study schools

School	Observations	Teachers interviewed	Pupils interviewed	Documents
A	Year 1 Year 2	Year 1 teacher Year 2 teacher Headteacher	Year 1: 2 girls and 2 boys Year 2: 2 girls and 2 boys	PSE document Behaviour policy Ofsted Prospectus
B	Year 2/3 Year 5	Year 2/3 teacher Year 5 teacher Special Needs Coordinator	None	Ofsted Prospectus
C	Year 5/6	Year 5/6 teacher PSE Coordinator	Year 5/6: 2 girls and 2 boys	Prospectus
D	Year 2 Year 5/6	None	Year 2: 2 girls Year 5/6: 1 boy and 1 girl	Prospectus
E	Year 3 Year 5/6	Headteacher Year 3 teacher Year 5/6 teacher	Year 3: 2 boys and 1 girl Year 5: 2 girls	Approach to managing discipline/behaviour
F	Year 1 + Reception Year 1/2	Year 1/Reception teacher Year 1/2 teacher	Year 1: 1 boy and 1 girl Year 2: 2 boys	Prospectus
G	None	Headteacher 3 nursery teachers	None	Ofsted Behaviour policy Equal opportunities policy PSE policy
H	Reception Year 5/6	Year 5/6 teacher Deputy Head Headteacher	Reception: 2 girls and 2 boys Year 5/6:2 girls and 2 boys	Prospectus Summary of Ofsted
I	Year 4 Bubble Time training	Year 3/4 teacher Year 4 teacher Headteacher	Year 4: 2 girls	Our approach to managing behaviour Prospectus Ofsted
J	Reception Year 3	Year 3 teacher Year 5 teacher Headteacher Deputy Head	Reception: 2 girls and 2 boys Year 3: 1 boy and 1 girl	School handbook Discipline policy Antibullying policy Ofsted

K	Nursery
	Year 1 +
	Reception
	Year 3/4
	  – two classes
	Staff meeting
	  with Family
	  Links
		Two Year 3/4
		teachers
			Two groups of 2 Year 3/4 girls	Prospectus
				Ofsted

L	Year 4 Year 5/6	Year 4 teacher Year 5/6 teacher	Year 4: 2 girls Year 6: 1 girl and 1 boy	Prospectus Policy document for PSE Ofsted
M	Year 2 – two Circle Times Year 5 – two Circle Times	Year 2 teacher Year 5 teacher	Year 2: 2 girls Year 5: 2 boys Year 2: 2 boys Year 5: 2 girls	Prospectus
N	Year 6	Year 6 teacher Acting Headteacher	Year 6: 2 girls Year 6: 2 boys	Aims of the school Ofsted Report

Appendix 2   Case-study schools and their Circle Time practices

School A

This quite new, denominational Infant and Nursery school in the north west of England had a suburban catchment area of broad social mix. There were 185 pupils aged between three and seven, with generally high academic ability. Fewer than ten per cent of the pupils were from ethnic minority groups or claimed free school meals. Positive policies and practices were in place to promote good behaviour and to enhance self-esteem and cooperation. The whole school had experienced Circle Time for two years. The school's Ofsted report commented: 'Positive attitudes are enhanced by the use of circle time where pupil's appreciate each other's strengths.' We interviewed the headteacher, observed Circle Time in a year 1 and a year 2 class and interviewed the teachers and two girls and two boys from each class.

School B

This First and Middle County school is situated in a large village in south central England and occupies extensive grounds. The pupils were aged from four to 12 and represented a complete range of academic ability. Fewer than ten per cent of pupils were from ethnic minority backgrounds or were receiving free school meals. An Ofsted report recognised the school's strong partnership with parents and the local community. The teachers were described as 'an efficient, caring team'. Pupils' moral and social development was also praised. The school had been using Circle Time for eight years from year 2 upwards. We observed a mixed year 2/3 class and a year 5 class and interviewed their teachers and the SEN coordinator. No pupils were interviewed.

School C

This large County Primary denominational school, situated in a medium sized town in the north west of England, was originally a middle and primary school on a shared site. It had 367 pupils, aged four to 11, representing a range of academic ability. Ten to 20 per cent of the pupils claimed free school meals and less than ten per cent were from ethnic minority groups. The school had not received a recent Ofsted inspection, but it appeared to have a range of PSE policies, provision and practices in place and was updating its RE and drugs education work schemes. The school prospectus refers to 'Personal and Social Education, often called Circle Time'. Three years earlier it had originally been used within the unit for children with dyslexia, but had then spread throughout key stage 2. We observed a mixed year 5/6 class and interviewed the teacher and the PSE coordinator, who conducted the session, and two girls and two boys.

School D

Situated in a suburban area of the central south this County Combined school catered for around 136 pupils aged four to 11. Between ten and 25 per cent of pupils received free school meals and fewer than ten per cent were from ethnic minority backgrounds. There were few or no students of very high ability. Circle Time had only been timetabled for one term although previously a visiting teacher specialising in Circle Time had used it with older pupils and a few other teachers had used it. We observed Circle Time sessions with a year 2 class and with a year 5/6 group and interviewed two year 2 girls and one girl and one boy from year 5/6. Time constraints during the visit did not permit teacher interviews.

School E

This Junior school in the east of England has a suburban catchment and 166 pupils, with a complete range of academic ability. Fewer than ten per cent of pupils were of ethnic minority background or claimed free school meals. The school was focusing on developing home-school liaison and improving school ethos with parental support. Circle Time had been used for 18 months throughout the school. The PSME policy was being developed to include Circle Time and other curricular and cross-curricular links were under review. Circle Time was also linked with the school's approach to behaviour, Learning for Life. We observed a year 3 class and year 5/6 class and interviewed the headteacher, the two class teachers, two boys and one girl from year 3 and two girls from year 5/6.

School F

This First School is situated to the west of London in a suburban area with strong community links and parental involvement. There were 238 pupils at the school, aged between five and nine, with a tendency towards a middle range of academic ability. There was also a nursery for three- to four-year-olds. Fewer than ten per cent of the pupils are of ethnic minority origin and 10–25% of pupils claim free school meals. Circle Time had been used for a couple of years, every week with key stage 1 and sometimes with key stage 2. We observed a mixed Reception and year 1 class and a mixed year 1/2 class. We interviewed their teachers, one boy and one girl from year 1 and two boys from year 2.

School G

This County Infant school is situated in a densely residential inner city location in central England, designated a social priority area, in which there is much unemployment. The junior school is located on the same site. Almost all of the 270 infant pupils (aged three to seven) are of Asian background, speak English as a second language and claim free school meals. The Asian community relates closely to the local mosque and has strong ties with Pakistan, but little involvement with the school. Long visits to Pakistan, poor attendance and lateness were noted in the school's Ofsted report, as also was the good behaviour of the children and that the school was 'a caring community', with 'a good positive ethos in the nursery', where 'they quickly make good progress in their personal and social development'. The senior nursery teacher had been using Circle Time for over six years, with the involvement of two or three other teachers. Unfortunately, due to the exceptional circumstances which occurred when we visited the school, we were unable to observe any Circle Time work, though we were able to interview the head and three nursery teachers.

School H

This Primary school is situated on a long-established site in the centre of a southern village. An Ofsted report described it as popular with parents, and the school prospectus stresses parental involvement. The school's rural catchment of 125 pupils, aged between four and 11, draws on a wide area. Fewer than ten per cent of the pupils claimed free school meals or were from ethnic minority groups. The school had a complete range of academic ability. Ofsted commended the pupils' social learning, sense of community and attitude to learning. Circle Time had been conducted as part of PSE by five teachers in the school for four years after one had been on an LEA INSET course on PSE and drama which included Circle Time. We observed the Reception class and a year 5/6 class, and interviewed the year 5/6 teacher and two girls and two boys from both these groups. We also had an extended conversation with the head and Reception teacher.

School I

This County Junior school had an urban situation in the East. It had 206 pupils, aged seven to 11, with an overall tendency towards low ability. There were around ten per cent of pupils of ethnic minority origin in the school and between 25–40 per cent were in receipt of free school meals. Circle Time had been in use by most of the teachers as part of behaviour management, developing school ethos and involving children in problem solving. It was intended to move towards a whole-school approach in PSE with more staff training. The school visit included two observations of Bubble Time training with year 4 pupils and teachers. We also interviewed the headteacher, the teachers of year 3/4 and year 4 classes, and two year 4 girls.

School J

The school is situated in a small rural market town in the north west. It has a wide catchment with a diverse social base. There were 227 pupils aged from three to 11 who represented a complete range of academic ability. There were almost no ethnic minority pupils and fewer than ten per cent of children were entitled to free school meals. The school's Ofsted report commended the school as 'a very good school with many strengths'. 'The provision of pupils' spiritual, moral, social and cultural development, the quality of teaching relationships between adults and pupils in the school are additional strengths.' Circle Time had been in use in the school for ten years. All but one teacher and some support staff actively used Circle Time as part of PSE. We observed Circle Time sessions in Reception and year 3 classes, and interviewed the year 3 teacher and two girls and two boys from Reception and one boy and one girl from year 3. We also interviewed a year 5 teacher who disliked Circle Time and no longer practised it, and had extended conversations with the headteacher and deputy head.

School K

This denominational First school located in an inner city situation in central England had 194 children aged three to 11. A complete range of academic ability was represented. There were between ten and 25 per cent of pupils who were from a range of ethnic minority and faith backgrounds. A similar percentage of pupils received free school meals. Circle Time had been in use as a whole-school approach for two years after training of all staff. It was used mainly as a means of conflict resolution, raising self-esteem and developing speaking and listening skills. The school's Ofsted report made two comments on Circle Time: 'There is a strong use of "Circle Time" where pupils have opportunities to discuss feelings and respect for others and the world' and 'Teachers encourage pupils to listen to other pupils' views in circle time and assemblies and they respond well to this'. We observed four Circle Time sessions (with Nursery, Reception and year 2, and two year 3/4 classes). We interviewed two year 3/4 teachers and two groups of two year 3/4 girls. We also observed a staff meeting which involved a family link project.

School L

A denominational Primary school set in a rural location in the east of England, this school served a mixed community. The 135 pupils aged from four to eleven years old, represented a complete range of academic ability. There were very few pupils from ethnic minority backgrounds. Between ten and 25 per cent of pupils received free school meals. The school's PSE policy emphasises the development of self-esteem and mentions that 'the school has purchased several "Circle-time" and discussion books as a resource for PSE sessions, structured in themes: the family; prejudice and difference, self-esteem and problem solving; community values and changes.' Ofsted commented 'The strongest area of the school's work is its contribution to the pupils' personal development.' Circle Time had been in use across the school by teachers and teaching assistants for five years with all groups once a week. We observed year 4 and year 5/6 groups in Circle Time and interviewed their teachers, two girls from year 4 and a girl and a boy from year 6.

School M

This denominational JMI school in south central England had a suburban catchment with fewer than ten per cent ethnic minority pupils. The school was proud of its Christian ethos, which was reflected in wall displays and the school's mission statement. There was an overall tendency in the school towards high academic ability. The school had 224 pupils, aged from four to 11, of whom fewer than ten per cent claimed free school meals. The teachers had been using Circle Time for about three years, mainly in the Nursery, Reception and years 1, 2 and 5 for a range of reasons, including building relationships and self-esteem. We visited the school on two occasions in one term and were thus able to observe a year 2 and year 5 class twice. We interviewed the year 2 and year 5 teachers and two girls and two boys from each class.

School N

This large County Junior school in south central England, with over 400 junior pupils, situated in a seaside town in the north west, had a complete range of academic ability and a broad social mix, though fewer than ten per cent ethnic minority pupils. The school was enhancing its citizenship programme, especially for year 6, inviting various members of the community into the school. The children were actively involved in making school rules and in a committee with school governors to investigate vandalism. Circle Time was seen as fitting in with other whole-school PSE initiatives, with the aim of discussing and building good relationships. Some staff (mostly year 4 teachers) had attended an LEA training course for Circle Time run by the PSHE adviser. There was an interest in getting other staff involved in Circle Time. The school's Ofsted report commended provision for SMSC opportunities and noted the pupils' engagement with developing school rules 'ensuring that pupils of all ages and abilities have a clear understanding of acceptable behaviour and the difference between right and wrong.' We interviewed the acting headteacher, a year 6 teacher and four year 6 pupils (two girls, two boys).

References

ANTI-BULLYING NETWORK (2002). *Information on Circle Time* [online]. Available: http://www. antibullying.net/circletime.htm [13 February, 2003].

ANTIDOTE (1998). 'Quality Circle Time: the heart of the curriculum.' *Conference Brochure of Jenny Mosley Quality Circle Time Model*, Westminster College, London, 25 June.

BALLARD, J. (1982). *Circlebook: a Leader Handbook for Conducting Circle Time. A Curriculum of Effect.* New York, NY: Rivington.

BLISS, T., ROBINSON, G. and MAINES, B. (1995). *Developing Circle Time.* Bristol: Lucky Duck Publishing.

BLISS, T. and TETLEY, J. (1993). *Circle Time: an Activity Book for Teachers.* Bristol: Lucky Duck Publishing.

BRANDES, D. and GINNIS, P. (1990). *The Student-Centred School.* Oxford: Blackwell Education.

BROPHY, J. (1981). 'Teacher praise: a functional analysis', *Review of Educational Research*, **51**, 1, 5–32.

BUTTON, L. (1976). *Outline Programme: Developmental Group Work.* Exeter: University of Exeter, School of Education, Action Research Project.

CAMPBELL, J. and DOMINY, J. (1997). 'Circle Time.' In: LLOYD, G. and MUNN, P. (Eds) *Sharing Good Practice. Prevention and Support Concerning Pupils Presenting Social, Emotional and Behavioural Difficulties.* Edinburgh: Moray House Publications.

CANFIELD, J. (1990). 'Improving students' self-esteem: a focus on academic and moral values', *Educational Leadership*, **48**, 1, 48–50.

CHAMBERLAIN, R. (1992). 'Ground rules: a case for their use in the classroom', *Pastoral Care in Education*, **10**, 4, 26–30.

COWIE, H. and SHARP, S. (1992). 'Students themselves tackle the problem of bullying', *Pastoral Care in Education*, **10**, 4, 31–7.

CREMIN, H. (2002). 'Circle Time: why it doesn't always work', *Primary Practice*, **30**, 23–8.

CRICK REPORT. DEPARTMENT FOR EDUCATION AND EMPLOYMENT. ADVISORY GROUP ON EDUCATION AND CITIZENSHIP AND THE TEACHING OF DEMOCRACY IN SCHOOLS (1998). *Education for Citizenship and the Teaching of Democracy in Schools*. London: QCA.

CURRY, M. (1997). 'Providing emotional support through circle-time: a case study', *Support for Learning*, **12**, 3, 126–9.

CURRY, M. and BROMFIELD, C. (1994). *Personal and Social Education for Primary Schools through Circle Time*. Stafford: NASEN.

CURRY, M. and BROMFIELD, C. (1998). *Circle Time: In-service Training Manual*. Stafford: NASEN.

DAMON, W. (1991). 'Putting substance into self-esteem: a focus on academic and moral values', *Educational Horizons*, **70**, 1, 13–17.

DAWSON, N. and McNESS, E. (1998). *A Report on the Use Of Circle-Time in Wiltshire Primary Schools*. Crediton: Jenny Mosley Consultancies.

DEPARTMENT FOR EDUCATION (1994). *Bullying – Don't Suffer in Silence. An Anti-bullying Pack for Schools*. London: DfE.

DEPARTMENT FOR EDUCATION AND EMPLOYMENT. NATIONAL ADVISORY GROUP ON PERSONAL, SOCIAL AND HEALTH EDUCATION (1999). *Preparing Young People for Adult Life: a Report by the National Advisory Group on Personal, Social and Health Education*. London: DfEE.

DIXON, D.A. (1981). *Teaching Children to Care*. Mystic, CT: Twenty-Third Publications.

DREIKURS, R. (1968). *Psychology in the Classroom*. New York, NY: Harper & Rowe.

EVANS, V. (1990). *Health Promoting Schools: a Training Manual*. Manchester: TACADE.

GALLAS, K. (1994). *Languages of Learning: How Children Talk, Write, Dance, Draw and Sing their Understanding of the World*. New York, NY: Teachers College Press.

GALLAS, K. (1997). *'Sometimes I Can Be Anything': Power, Gender and Identity in a Primary Classroom.* New York, NY: Teachers College Press.

GALTON, M. and FOGELMAN, K. (1998). 'The use of discretionary time in the primary school', *Research Papers in Education,* **13**, 2, 119–39.

GLASSER, W. (1969). *Schools without Failure.* New York, NY: Harper and Row.

GOLDTHORPE, M. and MOSELY, J. (1998). *Effective IEPs through Circle Time.* Wisbech: Learning Development Associates.

GOLEMAN, D. (1996). *Emotional Intelligence.* London: Bloombury.

HALL, K. (1995). 'Learning modes: an investigation of perceptions in five Kent classrooms', *Educational Research,* **37**, 1, 21–32.

HALL, S. (2002). 'Raising self-esteem: the key to school's dramatic turn around', *The Guardian,* 5 December.

HALSTEAD, J.M. and TAYLOR, M.J. (2000). *The Development of Values, Attitudes and Personal Qualities: a Review of Recent Research.* Slough: NFER.

HOUSEGO, E. and BURNS, C. (1994). 'Are you sitting too comfortably? A critical look at "circle time" in primary classrooms', *English in Education,* **28**, 2, 23–9.

KELLY, B. (1999).'"Circle Time": a systems approach to emotional and behavioural diffficulties', *Educational Psychology in Practice,* **15**, 1, 40–4.

LANG, P. (1996). 'Identifying Circle Time: its history, theory and practice.' Unpublished paper for workshop on 'The nature and value of Circle Time in schools and classrooms' at Affective Education Conference, Dublin, 29 May.

LANG, P. (1998). 'Getting round to clarity: what do we mean by Circle Time?' *Pastoral Care in Education,* **16**, 3, 3–10.

LANG, P. and MOSLEY, J. (1993). 'Promoting pupil self-esteem and positive school policies through the use of circle time', *Primary Teaching Studies,* **7**, 2, 11–15.

LOWN, J. (2002). 'Circle Time: the perceptions of teachers and pupils', *Educational Psychology in Practice,* **18**, 2, 93–102.

LUCAS, P. and JENKINS, S. (1988). 'Young children and issues-based discussion: some practical considerations', *Curriculum*, **9**, 2, 90–8.

MASLOW, A. (1968). *Towards a Psychology of Being*. New York, NY: Van Nostrand.

McLAUGHLIN, C. (2000). 'The emotional challenge of listening and dialogue', *Pastoral Care in Education*, **18**, 3, 16–20.

McMILLAN, J.H., SINGH, J. and SIMONETTA, L.G. (1994). 'The tyranny of self-oriented self-esteem', *Educational Horizons*, **72**, 3, 141–5.

MOORE, D.W., KNOTT, T. and McNAUGHTON, S. (1989). 'Pupil speech during morning news: the effects of reducing teacher questions and increasing pauses and praise', *Educational Psychology*, **9**, 4, 311–20.

MORENO, J.L. (1970). 'The Viennese origins of the encounter movement', *Group Psychotherapy*, **22**, 7–16.

MOSLEY, J. (1988). 'Some implications arising from a small-scale study of a circle-based programme initiated for the tutorial period', *Pastoral Care in Education*, **6**, 2, 10–17.

MOSLEY, J. (1992). 'Circle Time within a whole-school approach', *Primary Life*, **1**, 3, 19–23.

MOSLEY, J. (1993a). 'A whole-school approach to self-esteem and positive behaviour', *TOPIC*, Issue 9, Item 4.

MOSLEY, J. (1993b). *Turn Your School Round: a Circle-Time Approach to the Development of Self-Esteem and Positive Behaviour in the Primary Staffroom, Classroom and Playground*. Wisbech: Learning Development Aids.

MOSLEY, J. (1996). *Quality Circle Time in the Primary Classroom: Your Essential Guide to Enhancing Self-Esteem, Self-Discipline and Positive Relationships*. Wisbech: Learning Development Aids

MOSLEY, J. (1998a). *Photocopiable Materials for Use with the Jenny Mosely Circle Time Model*. Wisbech: Learning Development Aids.

MOSLEY, J. (1998b). Some Questions People Ask About Circle-Time. Unpublished report.

MOSLEY, J. (1998c). *The Whole School Quality Circle Time Model, 1986–1998: an Overview of Developments*. Trowbridge: Jenny Mosley Consultancies.

MOSS, H. and WILSON, V. (1998). 'Circle Time: improving social interaction in a Year 6 classroom', *Pastoral Care in Education*, **16**, 3, 11–17.

MYERS, J. (1998). 'Inside the circle', *Special!*, Spring, 34–5.

NEWTON, C. (1995). 'Circles of adults: reflecting and problem solving around emotional needs and behaviour', *Educational Psychology in Practice*, **11**, 2, 8–14.

QUALIFICATIONS AND CURRICULUM AUTHORITY (2000). *Personal, Social and Health Education and Citizenship at Key Stages 1 and 2: Initial Guidance for Schools*. London: QCA.

QUALIFICATIONS AND CURRICULUM AUTHORITY (2002). *Citizenship: a Scheme of Work for Key Stages 1 and 2*. London: QCA.

REED, L. (1998). 'Pupils take a circular route to good behaviour', *The Sunday Times*, 12 July, 25.

REICH, L.R. (1994). 'Circle Time in preschool: an analysis of educational praxis', *European Early Childhood Education Research Journal*, **2**, 1, 51–9.

ROGERS, C. (1983). *Freedom to Learn in the 1980s*. New York, NY: Macmillan.

TAYLOR, M.J. (2000). 'Values education: issues and challenges in policy and school practice.' In: LEICESTER, M., MODGIL, C. and MODGIL, S. (Eds) *Education, Culture and Values. Vol. 2. Institutional Issues: Pupils, Schools and Teacher Education*. London: Falmer Press.

TAYLOR, M. J., HILL, C. and LINES, A. (1998). Evaluation of the Citizenship Foundation's Primary School Materials, *You, Me, Us!*. Unpublished Report.

TEW, M. (1998). 'Circle Time: a much neglected resource in secondary schools?' *Pastoral Care in Education*, **16**, 3, 18–27.

TEW, M. (n.d) 'A Report on the Use of Jenny Mosley Whole School Quality Circle Time Model In Primary Schools in the UK. Unpublished report.

THACKER, J., STOATE, P. and FEEST, G. (1992) *Group Work Skills: Using Group Work in the Primary Classroom*. Crediton: Southgate.

TIMMERMAN, W. and BALLARD, J. (1975) *Strategies in Humanistic Education*. Milton, MA: Mandala.

WALD, P., MORRIS, L. and ABRAHAM, M. (1996). 'Three keys for successful Circle Time: responding to children with diverse abilities', *Dimensions of Early Childhood*, Winter, 26–9.

WHITAKER, P., BARRATT, P., JOY, H., POTTER, M. and THOMAS, G. (1998). 'Children with autism and peer group support: using "circles of friends"', *British Journal of Special Education*, **25**, 2, 60–4.

WHITE, M. (1990). 'Circletime', *Cambridge Journal of Education*, **20**, 1, 53–6.

WHITE, M. (1991). *Self-esteem: Promoting Positive Practices for Responsible Behaviour: Circle-Time Strategies for Schools, Set A*. Cambridge: Daniels Publishing.

WHITE, M. (1998a). *Magic Circles: Building Self-esteem through Circle Time*. Bristol: Lucky Duck Publishing.

WHITE, M. (1998b). *Picture This: Guided Imagery for Circle Time*. Bristol: Lucky Duck Publishing.

WOODCRAFT FOLK (1995). Leader Trainer Packs. (13, Ritherdon Road, London SW 17 8QE).